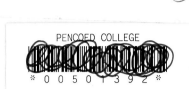

Novice to
Advanced
Dressage

Novice to Advanced Dressage

LÉONIE M. MARSHALL

J. A. Allen
London

British Library Cataloguing-in-Publication Data.
A catalogue record for this book is available from the British Library

ISBN 0.85131.631.X

First published 1981
Reprinted 1987
Revised edition 1996

Published in Great Britain in 1996 by
J. A. Allen & Company Limited,
1 Lower Grosvenor Place, Buckingham Palace Road,
London, SW1W 0EL

Typeset by Textype Typesetters, Cambridge
Printed by Dah Hua Printing Press Co., Hong Kong

Designed by Judy Linard

Contents

Preface   9
Introduction   11

Part 1
Conformation   13
Temperaments   14

Part 2
Preliminary and Novice Standard   15
How to feel when the balance is right   16
Riding in the arena   17
Learning to feel the gaits   21
Improving the rhythm of the gaits   23
Making the horse straight   25
Transitions and on the bit   26
How to achieve head flexion and uniform curve   29
Increasing the uniform curve   31
Circles and turns   33
Understanding impulsion and activity   36
Lightening of the forehand   38
Unlevelness   39
Halts and transitions   42
How much obedience to expect and
   how to achieve it   43
Gathering of the hind legs and start of piaffe   43
Lengthening the trot   44
Beginning the counter canter   45
Riding with one hand – 'giving' the rein   48
Improving the transitions   49

The rider   51
BHS Novice Test No 12   52

Part 3
Elementary and Advanced Elementary Standard   57
Impulsion and balance   58
Stiffness and hollowing the back   59
Improving shoulder-in   61
Commencing gait variations   64
Improving the outline   68
Preparation and positioning   70
Resistances (temperaments)   72
More circles   77
Developing counter canter   79
Pirouettes in walk   81
Leg yield   82
Half pass   84
The rein-back   86
BHS Elementary Test No 23   87

Part 4
Medium and Advanced Medium Standard   94
Collection – how to obtain the feel   95
Extension   95
Making the canter straight   97
Flying changes   97
Halt from canter   99
Half pass in canter   100
Pirouettes   101
Direct transitions – simple change   103
Medium and extended gaits   104
Use of spurs and the double bridle   105

Part 5
Advanced and Grand Prix Standard   107
Beginning piaffe   108
Improving walk pirouettes   109
Travers and renvers   110
Pirouettes in canter   113
Consecutive canter changes   116
Counter change of hand   117

Beginning passage   118
Gadgets   119
Conclusion   120

Preface

I am sure that competitors are often intrigued and perhaps worried by the thought of the judge behind the C marker. What goes on in their minds? Are they annoyed by a bad performance, amused by your futile attempts, or sympathetic to the difficulties.

As a judge I will not say I have never laughed! There can be amusing incidents, from the horse who left the arena during every movement, to the pony who would not leave even after the 60 seconds resistance, by which time he was eliminated!

However, judging is normally a serious business and the judge must, of necessity, possess good powers of concentration, his mind is trained to evaluate one fault against another and to weigh the good and bad.

If he is a rider, the problems facing the competitor will be known only too well, and the difficulties felt. The judge will know which faults are more easily corrected and which may need long term improvement. His judgement will be based on this knowledge. He will encourage in his marks or comments those riders whose basic training is correct, even though faults may occur. Riders who have not grasped the essential ingredients for producing a systematically trained horse will find their marks reflect their lack of knowledge. They may be disappointing or even upsetting, but judges do not give low marks or hard comments lightly. They are there to evaluate not destroy, to judge and not to teach, and they try to be as helpful as possible. Riders should appreciate the judges' difficulties, such as the relative speed with which they must make a comment and give a mark in order to keep up with the rider through the test.

This book is intended to enlighten the competitor to what the judge is looking for and how to try to arrive at that way of going.

Léonie Marshall

Introduction

This book is directed primarily towards ordinary riders, riders who, at the point when they first become interested in training their horse, may or may not aspire to riding tests, or indeed anything very much at all.

Training horses in a systematic way and developing their powers mentally and physically is a fascinating and absorbing occupation which, when discovered, may lead riders on to further effort and new interest. In turn, this interest often leads to an ambition to compete, either in a low or high sphere.

Until doors are opened to learning it is not always apparent how much there is to learn, a fact that is made perfectly plain when trying to train your horse.

A natural ability to ride, feel and understand the horse is a gift not given to all, and those fortunate enough to possess it may become ambitious early on in their riding career.

Those who do not have such an ability need a good deal of the right sort of help and a lot of perseverance to continue despite seemingly impossible forces! These riders need not despair. They may even end up further up the ladder than their gifted counterparts who, when things become sticky, fall by the wayside. It is surprising how much you can achieve with dogged determination and hard work.

The road from Novice to Grand Prix is hundreds of miles long, with many twists and turns, pitfalls and stumbling blocks. The end never seems in sight and if a rider is a perfectionist it can be a never-ending path.

However, with the interest and desire, most riders with quite ordinary horses can aim at the top and achieve most things, as I have been encouraged to discover during my teaching years.

Who knows, after all, who will end up at the Olympic Games? It has to be someone, and it could just be you.

Part 1

Conformation

Although most of us are not in a position to choose a horse with perfect conformation, there are some things which we can try to avoid if wishing to train to anything other than a fairly low level.

To start with, horses which are thick at the point where the head joins the neck should be avoided; they are often unable to flex to any great extent.

A long-necked horse can be a disadvantage because it bends at a point half-way down the crest instead of arching up from the withers.

A very short neck may also be a disadvantage because the horse will almost certainly look longer behind the saddle than in front, and may also be unable to arch his neck sufficiently.

A swan neck can be improved by a good rider but if the neck comes forward from behind the wither, the horse will find it almost impossible to raise it to an arched position, without a bulge forming underneath the neck.

An excessively long-backed horse will find it difficult to engage his hindquarters. A very short-backed horse, is difficult to sit on, and may find spinal curvature difficult in the lateral work.

Horses with the hind legs built under the body have a great advantage over those who have them out behind. Also, a horse who does not bend the joints of the hind legs actively looks more idle than one who does!

A horse who does not move with a free shoulder will have difficulty with extension, and one which is built higher behind than in front may find that it is too much of a problem when being asked to lower the hindquarters and lighten the forehand.

It may be true to say that any horse can be schooled to quite a high degree, even with the aforementioned problems, but there is no doubt that, as with top class athletes and dancers, the horse needs not only physical development but also to be structurally correct for the job.

Temperaments

If the horse has all the right conformation attributes then, to be consistently successful, his temperament must match his physical ability. Because every horse reacts differently to different problems, it is probably impossible to say what would be an ideal temperament for dressage.

Horses who learn very quickly are nicer to teach but may not be the best in the long run because they also learn the wrong things very quickly too.

Slow learners are sometimes ultimately the most obedient as they do not bother to think of ways out, but they can be frustrating to teach and sometimes dull.

Idle horses are often unwilling, and problems occur because they do not want to work. Nappy horses frequently emerge from this category and, although much can be done, a horse who has learned to nap may let his rider down in a moment of crisis however well he has been reschooled.

Perhaps it would be safe to say that a horse who likes to go forward naturally is generally nice to train because he is not antiwork and, as long as his natural impulse allows restraint by the rider, without resentment or tension, then horse and rider can come to a good working arrangement.

Part 2

Preliminary and Novice Standard

JUDGES' REQUIREMENTS
At this level the judges would like to see a balanced horse who is capable, through obedience and suppleness, of maintaining a steady outline and head carriage with regular, active and rhythmic gaits.

FAULTS WHICH LOSE THE MOST MARKS
Crookedness.
Wrong bends and stiffness.
Movements ridden incorrectly.
Lack of rhythm and balance.
Lack of impulsion/activity.
Being above the bit.
Rough transitions.
Overbending.
Resistance to aids.
Opening mouth.
Tongue out or over bit.
Grinding teeth.
Tail swishing.

How to feel when the balance is right

The rider must understand the importance to himself and his horse of being able to balance and maintain the balance on a straight line and around corners.

An unbalanced horse cannot perform easily because he is constantly battling with his own, and his rider's, weight and, if he is having difficulty, resistance is inevitable.

The rider must realise that the forehand is the heaviest part of the horse and that the weight will remain there unless something is done about it.

An unbalanced horse may be recognised in several different ways: he may pull, lean on the hand, throw his head up, twist his head, lean over on the corners and circles, swing the hindquarters, trip, forge, wander from side to side, be unable to maintain a steady gait, resist the aids, have incorrect spinal flexion, and so on.

The novice rider may feel his horse is balanced when he has made a gait steady so that the horse can maintain it without constant correction, can keep his head steady with a quiet mouth, can make transitions smoothly and go round corners without quickening the stride and keeping the correct curve.

The rider may use small half halts to achieve the balance of the gaits and to take weight off the forehand. These half halts take the form of a 'steady' given gently by the hands and supported by the legs so that the horse maintains a regular gait.

The rider must maintain a good position in the saddle, avoid moving his body about and altering the weight which will cause the horse to change his. He must especially avoid leaning sideways, and/or forwards, swinging his legs, bumping in the saddle and jerking the contact on the horse's mouth.

Good balance is essential to a good performance, and to the whole of the horse's training.

Riding in the arena

If the rider is to train a horse satisfactorily, he must spend a lot of time working in an arena, so the first thing to do is to learn how to use the arena at his disposal.

The usual arena is 20 m × 40 m (see Fig. 1) or 20 m × 60 m (see Fig. 2) consisting of four straight sides and four corners. The arena is marked with letters to enable the rider to ride the school movements accurately.

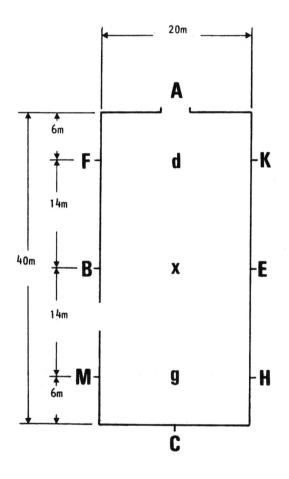

Fig. 1 Dressage arena – 20 m × 40 m

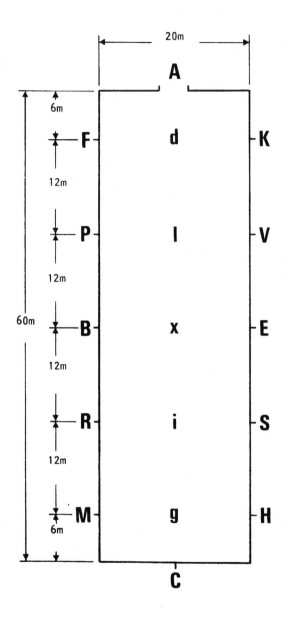

Fig. 2 Dressage arena – 20 m × 60 m

18

The rider must ensure that the horse is straight on the sides and curved in the corners, in the direction in which he is going. This lesson may take some time because, although it sounds simple, it is incredibly difficult to do well. The rider may need to look down occasionally at the neck of the horse to see that it is straight, and also watch the ears to make sure that there is no tilt of the head. If the forehand is straight, the hindquarters should follow, but the hindquarters may fall in or out and the rider must correct this by riding forward more for a moment and making the contact of leg and hand more even.

The rider should try to ride all four corners the same consistently, aiming for a point on the track before the corner and another after the corner, the in-between piece being a curve the size of which is determined by the state of training of the horse. The rider must not bend the neck to achieve the corner because this is a false bend. The whole length of the horse must curve slightly, achieved by the use of the rider's inside leg being used strongly into the outside rein and being supported by the other hand and leg. The outside leg will also prevent the hindquarters falling out and maintain the spinal curve round the inside leg; the inside hand will ask for a slight lateral flexion.

Next the rider must learn how to change direction in such a way that the horse can remain in balance and maintain his rhythm and outline. There are several school movements which enable the rider to do this but the first one to tackle is changing the rein on the diagonal (see Fig. 3). (Novice riders may confuse this with the diagonals in trot which is explained on page 22.)

To teach the change of rein on the diagonal, the rider must ride the short side of the school and turn across exactly at the quarter markers, ensuring that the corner is ridden correctly prior to the change of rein and starting on the long side so that the horse is straight momentarily before turning. He must also have been prepared for leaving the track before the quarter marker by the rider asking for a slight lateral head flexion towards the direction of travel, but not allow-

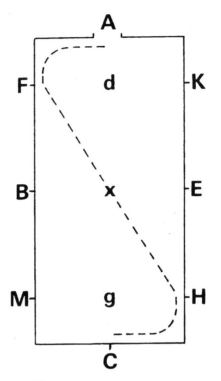

Fig. 3 Change rein on the diagonal

ing the horse to turn until he reaches the marker. Once on the diagonal the horse must be straight and only as the rider approaches the quarter marker on the opposite side should the new flexion be taken preparatory to riding the next corner.

Circles, 20 m in diameter, are the next most simple movement to ask of the horse and rider (see Fig. 4). With novices it is probably best to walk the route first riding to the points of the circle, i.e. if the circle starts at C, the track should be touched between the quarter and half markers on the long sides and the rider should go through X.

Before the circle is begun the preparatory aids must be given, i.e. the head is flexed in the direction of travel, and

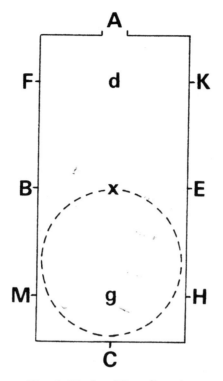

Fig. 4 Circle – 20 m diameter

then on the circle the spinal flexion is maintained. Most novice riders will have more bend in the horse's neck than in the rest of the body and will be unable to keep the correct curve round the circle. Only when they have learned more about achieving flexion and making the horse yield to the leg instead of lying against it, will they improve.

Learning to feel the gaits

THE WALK
The rider should proceed in walk round the school or arena on a long rein, so that the horse can walk out with his head

21

and neck stretched forward. The rider should then try to assess in his mind the feel of the length of the strides which should be as long and natural as possible with the hind feet overtracking the imprint of the forefeet. This length should be maintained when contact is taken so that there is no restriction on the part of the rider. Even when the horse is asked to come on the bit the rider must feel no shortening of the stride and no stiffening of the back under his seat.

THE TROT

When beginning in trot, the first thing to achieve is a speed at which the horse can maintain a steady rhythm with the maximum possible balance. Horses can generally only learn to produce a rhythm when ridden quite slowly to start with, and the rider will probably have to constantly correct the steps to arrive at the right speed for the horse. The rhythm will then begin to show itself, if it is not already present, and the rider will start to feel a steady tempo and must then aim to produce a little suspension or lift within the trot by making sure that the horse is active. The rider must strive to maintain a good even contact with his legs and hands in order to keep the horse in regular and even steps, and straight.

DIAGONALS

The horse's trot is a two-time gait, e.g. the off-fore and nearhind coming to the ground together, followed by the near-fore and off-hind; the rider rising as one pair of legs comes to the ground and sitting when the other pair comes to the ground. To determine the correct diagonal upon which to sit, the rider may (when learning) briefly glance down to the outside foreleg (not leaning forwards) and if he can see it coming forward, he should aim to sit in the saddle as it comes to the ground. If he desires to change his diagonal he must sit for one extra stride and then carry on rising.

Most teachers ask their pupils to sit in the saddle when the inside hind leg and outside foreleg come to the ground, in order to balance the horse on circles and corners, but the most important point is that the diagonal should be changed when changing the rein in order to develop the horse's muscles evenly. Riders should try to feel any one-sidedness which might occur if the horse begins to curve more on one side than the other.

THE CANTER

The rider probably cannot feel the three-time beat of the canter easily unless his horse is fairly well trained and balanced. Usually the first step is for the rider to know which leg he is on and with some people this takes considerable time. They may have to glance down to see if the inside foreleg is coming forward in front of the shoulder, or they try to feel the lift of the shoulder that the horse usually makes preparatory to the strike-off.

Having achieved the correct leading leg, the rider has to try to achieve a steady canter which he can sustain on corners and circles without losing balance. He must then look for a rhythm of stride, and try to feel that his horse has a moment of suspension between one stride and the next, and that the canter does not merge into one surging rush forward with little control.

Improving the rhythm of the gaits

STARTING HALF HALTS

The trot and canter are usually the two gaits at which the rhythm can obviously be at fault, although the walk can also be hurried or uneven. On the whole the walk is best left alone as much as possible. Many walks are spoilt by the horse being brought together too soon.

To be able to improve rhythm it is generally necessary, temporarily, to reduce impulsion, allowing the horse to learn to control his limbs at a slow speed in a relaxed way. He must be calm because any muscle tension will prevent the harmony and rhythm of the steps which should blend smoothly together.

If the gait at which the rider is working is hurried, lacks balance and the horse is pulling, the rider must endeavour to slow down.

The rider must then concentrate on the rhythm required, two-time in trot and three-time in canter, counting the foot falls either silently or out loud if it helps. Some work on a hard surface will soon enable the rider to tell the beat of the foot falls, even in canter.

To achieve the right speed the rider will have to use checking aids or minor half halts to slow the horse's speed with the hand, ensuring that his legs are there to prevent the horse changing his gait or becoming lazy.

Novice riders find it difficult to co-ordinate hand and leg; it takes practice before the right amount of hand is used which does not alter the head carriage or interrupt the stride for too long causing loss of rhythm instead of improvement.

HALF HALTS FOR THE NOVICE HORSE
At the rider's request the horse must shorten his steps for a moment giving him time to collect himself a little. The rider must hold the posture for a few steps so that when he *eases* the rein again the horse will keep himself in balance and not fall forward onto the bit. The rider must not *release* the rein because this allows the horse to come off the bit and everything which has been gained is wasted.

When using these checking or rebalancing aids it is most important to keep the horse straight because crookedness will cause unlevelness of stride or one-sidedness.

Rhythm is something which should come from the rider, only a few horses have it 'built in', so their concentration and constant correction in the early stages is essential to establishing this vital basic ingredient.

Making the horse straight

This has been mentioned already in Riding in the Arena but because it is of such importance, the rider may like a little more detail.

It is vital that the horse should be capable of going in straight lines so that he can develop his balance and control, and to ensure that his muscles are equally strong on both sides. A one-sided horse is uncomfortable to ride and cannot perform to maximum effect. Most horses appear to be one-sided and will naturally put up resistance when asked to do anything on their difficult side. Riders must know this fact so that they can be prepared for difficulties and accept that the horse will take longer to do what they ask on that rein.

The rider should feel that the horse is straight when the acceptance of the bit is even on both sides. If the horse's neck remains straight, the body will follow without the hindquarters swinging.

When on a curve the acceptance of the bit must be even, the neck curved only as much as the rest of the horse, with the hind legs following the track of the forelegs.

The horse will possibly resist straightness owing to some stiffness which has been caused by the rider. In walk and trot the rider must constantly correct him so that eventually he will keep himself straight. In canter, if the horse is very crooked, it may be necessary for the rider to put the horse into a minor degree of shoulder-in (see page 31) because only by correcting the forehand can the hindquarters follow. The shoulder-in aids will help bring the forehand in very slightly, the rider using the inside leg rather firmly to prevent the horse coming off the track. Someone on the ground standing at the end of the long side of the school will be able to tell the rider whether he has achieved the straightening. If the horse is not made to go straight in canter, all sorts of irritating things can go wrong and he will not be able to progress.

Many novice riders pull the horse round by the inside

25

rein in the corners of the arena in canter. Not only is this unbalancing for the horse but it also causes loss of control of the outside shoulder, and sometimes makes the horse change legs or become disunited.

If either of these problems occur the rider must check his own, and his horse's, ability to go straight. Riders should understand that a horse performs best when he can see where he is going and it is up to his 'pilot' to make sure he does this, so that the rest of his body can follow without difficulty.

Transitions and on the bit

A transition is a change of gait, e.g. walk to trot, trot to canter, or it can be a change within the gait, e.g. working to medium.

At Novice level we are only really concerned with changes from one gait to another except in trot when some lengthening is required.

Wherever a transition has to be made it is important that the horse is absolutely straight. Riders must make sure that their horse's head and neck are straight, that the ears are level and that the hindquarters are not over to one side or swinging from side to side. The next thing to watch is that the head carriage remains steady and that the rhythm of the previous gait is maintained until the new gait is asked for, at which time the rhythm of that gait must be established, the whole thing blending into an almost effortless manoeuvre. In an upward transition the horse must respond instantly to the given aid which should be light and, if not obeyed immediately, supported by the schooling whip so that the horse learns to answer at once.

In downward gait transitions, resistance is quite likely as the balance is difficult to get exactly right with a novice horse and his head may go up, his back may hollow and he will probably fall on the forehand, especially from canter to trot. The improvement to this transition will probably take some time and riders must not despair. They must endeavour to improve the control they have in the canter, trying to slow it down and keep it balanced, so that when the horse breaks into trot not too much balance is lost. Also, if the transition is as slow as possible, the rider is not thrown about thus losing his position and control, and can regain his balance more quickly. The transition will not be smooth until the horse accepts the bit and will go forward into trot without resistance. Inexperienced riders find this very difficult at first and it is best to try to get them to improve the trot to walk, and walk to halt, to get the feel of the bit acceptance and to give the horse the feel too.

At this point, if the novice horse has not already learned to accept the bit thoroughly, now is the time to improve because no transition will be really easy until there is complete acceptance of the hand aids.

I have always remembered what my Riding Master said to me about acceptance of the bit. He said: 'If you've got the mouth, you've got the lot'. A fairly caustic comment and it took me a long time to understand exactly what it meant, and a good deal longer to learn how to achieve it, but I have come to realize how right he was and what a vital point he was trying to make.

Experienced riders will teach their horses to come on the bit or to accept the hand from the word go, but it is much harder for novices to do because, even if they have the understanding, it takes a while to develop the feel.

Initially, the rider must try to understand what he is trying to get the horse to do. It may be explained in many ways, but this is one method. Start at halt and ask the horse to come on the bit by closing the legs to prevent the horse from reversing away from it, then applying some pressure evenly on the horse's mouth. The result you hope for is that the horse will flex at the poll, bringing his nose just in front of the vertical, and relax his lower jaw, giving to the pressure.

The rider must recognise when this happens by watching the poll, and by feeling a yield and possibly a slight chewing on the bit. As soon as the horse responds, the rider must lighten the pressure and hold it gently and evenly.

The horse will learn to keep his head in the most comfortable place and will eventually come into position from a light pressure. At first he will resist the pressure and nothing will be achieved unless the rider persistantly maintains his hold until a yield occurs.

The difficult part is to then proceed into walk maintaining the amount of give obtained at the halt. The natural impulse of the horse will be to raise his head or pull forwards. The rider may then have to be really firm in his pressure on the bit to obtain the yield, but must be concentrating to such an extent that he can lighten immediately to any response made by the horse. Only in this way can the horse learn what is wanted. A pat on the neck with one hand is also very effective to reward the horse, but contact must be maintained by the other hand.

If the rider learns to keep his horse on the bit in walk, he must then work on the transition into trot, and again into walk, only going a short distance between the transitions which will enable him to keep the desired contact.

He can then bring the horse into halt again making sure he stays straight and does not step back. Most riders forget to use their legs when riding into halt thus allowing hindquarters to swing, or halts which are not square.

Work on the canter transition may be done when the other transitions are as smooth as possible.

The rider must understand the canter aids and know that the most effective way to start a young horse on the correct leg is in a corner. It is important to be able to sit to the trot without bumping about and to control the trot, not allowing it to accelerate as the aids are given. The inside leg is applied on the girth, the outside leg behind the girth. The inside rein gives the directional aid and the outside rein controls the speed. The horse must respond immediately to the given aid and strike off with the inside foreleg leading.

The rider must then remember to steer straight, keep the horse balanced and not allow the horse to trot until he is told to do so.

Another transition required in Novice tests is that from working trot to lengthened strides and back to working trot. The rider must know that in order to achieve lengthening, the horse must first be well balanced, straight and accepting the bit. He is trying to lengthen the strides by closing his legs and keeping them firmly on the horse to keep up impulsion, and by maintaining a firm contact on the horse's mouth. He must not release the reins to achieve the lengthening.

The horse's steps must increase in length but the rhythm must not speed up and he must make the transition to the lengthening and return to working trot without hurrying or becoming abrupt. The horse can only do this if he has his hind legs under him and enough impulsion.

It is advisable at this standard to teach the horse to make a transition from trot to halt through walk so that any resistance to the aid is minimised; the horse is also more likely to remain straight.

The rider must try to feel what the horse's hind legs are doing in the final stages of the walk so that he knows where each one has stopped, and can ask the horse to move forward any leg which is left behind.

How to achieve head flexion and uniform curve

HEAD FLEXION
The horse must yield primarily to two things, the hands and, laterally, the legs.

To achieve a yield to the hand the novice rider may try to feel evenly on the horse's mouth having first held him with the legs, and wait until he gives to the bit. He may find that there is resistance to this request and may need to be more demanding to get his result. To teach the rider to know the stiff side of the horse the instructor may ask him to feel on one side endeavouring to achieve a flexion of the head only on that side of the horse's mouth. He should feel some mobility or slight chewing of the bit. The flexion may be asked for before circles and turns to 'start' the curve which must then be taken up by the leg.

When riding on a straight line, pupils can practise keeping the horse's legs on a straight line but flexing his head one way or the other. The horse must not wobble. The rider must learn to use variations of tension on the rein so that the horse is not fixed in a position, but almost holds the position himself until the request is modified by the rider.

UNIFORM (SPINAL) CURVE

The yield to the leg may be more difficult, for both the horse and rider, because the rider must learn to put his leg against the horse and have some effect, and the horse must learn to be sensitive to a light aid. If horse and rider are learning together, the rider will almost certainly have to learn to use the schooling whip to help his leg. He must learn to turn his wrist sharply while holding the rein, contacting the flank behind the leg with the schooling whip, and making sure that he does not jerk the horse's mouth.

When the horse feels the whip he may flinch away from it and having used it a few times, the rider must then only use the leg to achieve the same reaction. He must do this on both reins until the horse will move a few steps away from each leg equally. At first, this exercise should be executed on a circle. The application of the aid must then become smooth so that the horse is not frightened but simply gives to the aid.

Some horses will take longer to respect the whip than others and may be quite stubborn in their resistance to its use. The rider should persevere, as a horse which will not accept the schooling whip is difficult to train.

Once the horse has learned to give to the leg, and will move away when the leg is applied, the rider must work to achieve a true spinal flexion which is a uniform curve of the horse from nose to tail. The hind legs must at all times follow the forelegs on the same track. The rider may prepare with a head flexion but, before circling, should increase the inside leg aid until he feels the amount of give he needs to get round the circle with no change in the overall flexion and no falling in.

When the inside rein and leg are used in this way, the rider must ensure that the tempo, and the direction of the line of the circle, is held by his outside hand, with the outside leg a little back to keep the hindquarters round his inside leg.

Increasing the uniform curve

When rider and horse understand the preliminary aids and the horse will give a little to hand and leg, then the way to improve the spinal curvature and give the rider a better idea of the control of the forehand, is to teach shoulder-in (see Fig. 5).

Stand the horse on the track facing one end of the school, and ask him to move only the forefeet in off the track by keeping the inside leg on the girth to prevent the horse moving in too far and keeping the outside leg behind the girth to stop the hindquarters going out.

The inside rein is held a little away from the neck, and the outside rein on the neck, or no movement of the forehand will be achieved.

Having positioned the horse, the rider must try to hold the position and make the horse move sideways at walk from the inside leg, using the schooling whip to help. He must aim to keep the horse on three tracks: inside foreleg, outside foreleg and inside hind leg together, and outside hind leg. Having taught the horse how to hold the position and obey the aids in walk, the horse must be asked to trot slowly and try to achieve the same thing. Experienced riders will know that a degree of collection should be

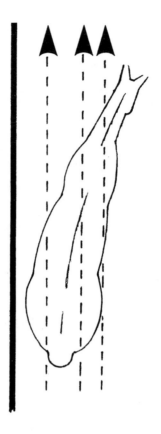

Fig. 5 Shoulder-in

accomplished before a true shoulder-in can be carried out, but novice riders and horses can only expect a small degree at a slow speed to start with. Sometimes it may even be necessary to start in walk and then push the horse into a slow trot while in the position for shoulder-in; because it is so slow, rider and horse can control the angle they have.

The rider must not allow the following faults to occur:

1. The outside shoulder falling out. Prevent this with the outside rein and leg. If the shoulder falls back onto the track, slow up a little and reposition.
2. Too much bend in the neck. The rider must try to use his reins evenly with the outside rein against the neck and

only a light feel on the inside rein for the flexion. If the neck bend becomes pronounced, begin again as the shoulder-in position has been lost.

3. Head tilting. Sometimes the horse will evade the aid by twisting his head. This can become a very tiresome habit. Try to feel this happening and correct the unevenness of the rein contact and the acceptance of the bit so that they are equal. Watch the horse's ears, one will often be lower than the other when the horse is trying to tilt his head.

4. Too much or too little angle. The horse must be on three tracks as previously explained and this is the angle to hold. Novices will find it difficult to start with, but when carried out correctly this exercise is extremely valuable, giving both horse and rider a much better degree of control.

Once the shoulder-in has been taught it should be easier for the rider to make his horse flex better on a circle and corners, etc. Although not specifically asking for shoulder-in, if the rider uses the aids and thinks 'shoulder-in', to a minor degree, the control and curvature must be better.

Circles and turns

At Novice level the size of circles should be larger rather than smaller. To make a young or untrained horse go round a small circle, will cause him to become unbalanced, resulting in many difficulties, such as unlevelness, change in rhythm, unsteady head carriage and so on.

If there is a 40 m × 20 m arena available the rider should aim to ride his circle at one end of the arena or in the centre (see Figs. 6 and 7).

There should be four points to each circle (see Figs. 6 and 7) and these points must be carefully ridden with the horse curved to the line of the circle.

He must not bend the neck more than the rest of his body and he must maintain the spinal curvature all the way

33

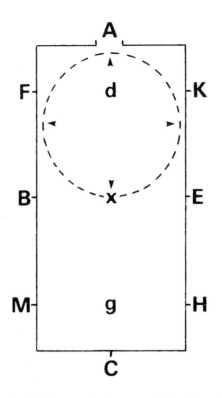

Fig. 6 Circle at end of arena – 20 m diameter

round the circle.

Before riding the circle the rider must take a lateral head flexion with the inside hand so that the horse is ready. When he leaves the track the rider must hold the horse to the circle with the outside hand and the inside leg, asking for the flexion with the inside hand and curving the hindquarters round the inside leg with the outside leg. It all sounds rather complicated because a novice rider must think of each hand and leg to start with, but he will gradually find that the four entities can become co-ordinated to work together from one thought.

Apart from circles it will be necessary to teach the horse

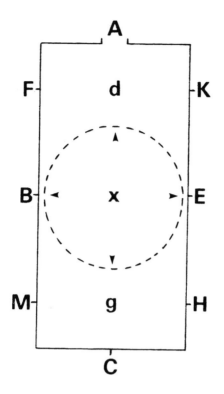

Fig. 7 Circle in centre of arena – 20 m diameter

to perform turns at A, C, B and E. On each occasion the rider must take a slight lateral head flexion first and then make the turn a little before the marker. As soon as the turn is made the rider must aim for the opposite marker going near enough to it to make a turn without interrupting the stride. (see Fig. 8).

The aids are the same as those for circles. The rider must avoid turning on the inside rein alone as this will cause the horse to fall onto the inside shoulder and will prevent a true curve. He must think always of inside leg to outside hand, the inside hand being as light as possible. The outside leg giving good support to the hindquarters.

35

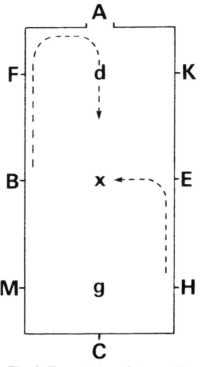

Fig. 8 Turn at A, and turn at E

Understanding impulsion and activity

These two words, impulsion and activity, probably cause as much confusion as any, as most riders tend to confuse them with speed. It has nothing to do with rushing the horse forward. In fact, if this happens, true impulsion is never really achieved.

The first essential is to ride the horse slowly in a very steady rhythm so that he is relaxing mentally and physically. In this state he will be able to use his hind legs under his body enabling him to carry the load and bring about the lightening of the forehand.

Although the speed is quite slow the horse should not be

36

allowed to be lazy and, if impulsion is to develop, the hind legs must be active. The joints must all flex and work so that the horse elevates himself a little at each stride as well as moving forward.

This activity is usually achieved best with the help of the long schooling whip which can be used if the horse is idle to make him step from one hind leg to the other with more energy.

The rider should feel this energy, through the sensitivity of his seat, and should recognise it by the fact that the horse desires to go forward himself without being constantly driven, and has enough energy to perform no matter what he is asked to do.

At Novice level, the impulsion is relative to the requirements and will at this stage be less powerful than will be needed later.

The rider must assess whether his horse is able to do what is being asked easily. If it is too laboured, then more activity of the hind legs is necessary. If, on the other hand, the horse cannot hold the rhythm on the corners or in the circle, he may well have too much energy which must be reduced temporarily.

Horses vary so much. Some will naturally be lazy and a good deal of 'stick' may be needed to persuade them to work. The rider will need to be very disciplined with himself and the horse to make sure he does make the horse work. He will not like to hit him but he may have to, at first, until the horse understands that he must go forward.

These horses very often 'kick' at the schooling whip, and I am afraid that there is only one way to stop this: to carry on using it until they stop! If the rider gives up, the horse will know that he only has to kick out and he will not have to do what he is told.

A naturally impulsive horse is hard to ride because the rider must be very patient and calm. The horse will have to be made to go slowly and must relax so that he is receptive to learning. If his natural impulsion is handled with skill, he may well be the better horse in the end as he will always have the ability and desire to go forward which will be a help to the rider when he and the horse have learned to control it.

Lightening the forehand

Although there has been a lot mentioned already about taking weight from the forehand, and although it is mentioned in other sections with balance, improving the gaits etc., it is such an important factor that I would like to dwell on it for a moment longer.

There is a lot talked about young or novice horses being allowed to go in a long low outline, and over the years I wonder if this has been correctly done. I imagine that the original intention was to prevent riders from trying to bring their horses into a more advanced shape too soon involving a certain amount of force, which in turn would damage the muscles not yet strong enough to cope with the requests made.

Theoretically of course this idea of the long low outline sounds acceptable. However, I believe it has caused a great deal of disappointment to those who have tried to follow the idea without being fully aware of certain major factors, which I should now like to point out.

If the novice horse is to work forward freely, i.e. with his hind legs under his body propelling him actively, if his back is to be supple, and his head and neck slightly raised and arched, and if he is to accept the bit correctly, he cannot be allowed to have weight bearing down from the wither, through the shoulders and onto the forelegs. If it does he will be on the forehand and unable to accept the bit because he has to lean on it for support. His neck will become heavy as he leans, his back will become stiff because his mouth is not right, and the hindquarters cannot come under the body if there is stiffness in the back. The result? A vicious circle!

Riders should really take note of these points if they ever

want to be successful. A dressage horse which is on the forehand, will never attain those heights hoped for by his ambitious rider; it is physically impossible.

It is, therefore, never too early to start using small half halts (for principles of the half halt see page 70) to correct the balance, which will help to lighten the forehand. To use half halts the horse must accept the hand and it is never too soon to make that happen so long as the horse goes forward when the legs are used. The horse must respond immediately when the legs are applied and thereafter go forward without resistance using his hind legs actively.

If the rider thinks his horse is giving to the hands equally and accepting the bit, he should then use his legs and feel the response. If the horse goes forward straight away without any resistance to the leg or hand, the rider may keep him in short steps until the balance is level (no weight on the hands), and then ride the horse actively forward maintaining the lightness of the weight on the bit. If the weight should gradually tip forwards the rider should immediately reduce the speed and start the procedure again.

Unlevelness

Any unevenness or irregularity in the stride of any gait is fairly serious and will be marked down in tests. The rider must appreciate the reasons causing the unlevelness and then he will realise why it is so detrimental and why it needs to be corrected quickly before becoming confirmed.

Generally speaking unlevelness occurs owing to resistance to the bit and hands, but is also sometimes due to the horse being asked to do an exercise before he is ready, avoiding an even response to the legs, crookedness, muscles more developed on one side that the other, lost balance, rhythm not established, hindquarters insufficiently engaged, and a lack of impulsion. In fact it can be the result of a defect in any one of the basic essentials, thus showing a fault in the foundation upon which the rest of the work has to be built and which must be corrected.

Unlevelness may occur in front or behind. The horse will step short on one leg and longer with the others. The horse may appear lame in extreme cases.

The rider may feel the unlevelness if it is fairly bad, but novice riders may not be experienced enough to feel it and someone on the ground can very often help. If the horse is unlevel in front, it will be fairly obvious to the onlooker but if it occurs behind, it is more difficult to see except by a trained eye. The onlooker should first observe the length of the steps of the hind feet to see whether they overtrack evenly. Then the eye should go to the hocks to see if one comes higher than the other, and then from behind, the assistant should look at the hips and the hindquarters to see that both sides are even. If the muscles are developed un-evenly one hindquarter may be lower than the other.

With unlevelness in front, the rider must first improve the acceptance of the bit and then work to free and lengthen the stride of the leg which is 'going short'. Work in walk using lateral exercises, shoulder-in, half-pass, travers, renvers and pirouettes, will all help to supple the muscles causing the short stride.

The exercises also apply to unlevelness behind, including walk on a long straight line, using the schooling whip on the lazy leg.

Persistant unlevelness can be difficult to cure and, if there is a physiological reason, it may be impossible to cure. If the rider is in doubt or the condition does not improve with work, veterinary advice may be helpful as the horse may actually be lame or have some muscular damage or there could be other reasons.

Trot unlevelness in front is usually the result of a lack of balance and/or suppleness on corners, circles, etc., and manifests itself in an alternation of length of stride, loss of rhythm, loss of head carriage, and so on.

The horse will normally 'go short' on the inside foreleg, often appearing lame. Corrections must be made to the mouth, by making the bit acceptance more even, to the balance and to the lateral curvature of the whole horse. In addition one foreleg may come higher than the other. Generally this is because the horse is not straight, but he may also be wrong in the mouth.

If the horse takes uneven strides behind, the reason very often is that the muscles are unevenly developed. He will be quite considerably stiffer on one rein than the other. The shoulder-in exercise is valuable, if done correctly, for making the horse more supple and for making the appropriate inside hind leg work more under the body.

When the shoulder-in is equally good on both sides, the stiffness should disappear and the muscles which have been 'blocking' the short striding leg will relax and allow the leg to cover the same ground as the other.

Unlevelness of the hocks or hips may be due to some skeletal trouble, such as fusion of the vertebrae or low grade function of ligaments.

Sometimes the term 'bridle lame' is used when a horse is unlevel. When the mouth is corrected and the bit acceptance made even, the unlevelness usually disappears.

Unlevelness is more difficult to see in canter because of the three-time beat of the footfalls; the comparison of the legs is much more difficult.

In the past few paragraphs I have been talking mainly about continuous unlevelness, but there is also irregularity of stride which occurs for a few steps at a time and then the horse will become perfectly regular again.

These irregularities are usually due to momentary resistance, loss of balance, stiffness and/or evasion, which, although they must be corrected, are not major disasters if they only occur once or twice during the test. The judge will mark such mistakes down but will assess the degree of irregularity and its cause before giving the mark for that movement.

Halts and transitions

Bringing a young or novice horse into a square halt can be difficult, and obtaining smooth transitions from trot into halt for a test causes a lot of problems for riders and horses.

Firstly, I believe that the rider should think of the straightness of the horse and then of the progressiveness of the transition.

If the halt is straight but not square it is a reasonable beginning. When the horse has understood that he must stand calmly at halt and not fidget, then the rider can consider where the horse's legs are and whether the halt is square or not.

The rider must pay attention to his aids into halt, making certain that he keeps his legs on, he must not take them away, especially whilst in the halt. If the pressure is re-moved the horse will almost certainly step back from the bit pressure and the rider will have nothing between hand and leg.

To achieve a square halt the rider, having made sure he is straight, may try to correct an erring leg by tapping it with his schooling whip but care must be taken if the rider leans over to see the leg; the horse, feeling the change of weight, will almost certainly move. Increased pressure from the rider's leg on the appropriate side will in time make the horse square up. The best way to ensure a decent halt is to come into it on the bit.

The transitions should be gradual, especially to start with, and the rider should aim to come down to walk well before the place he wishes to halt, to give the horse a chance to rebalance himself if necessary.

Moving off from halt will, to start with, be into walk and then into trot, but I believe that even young horses should be made to be sharp to a light squeeze, therefore if the aid when applied is not answered directly, the schooling whip should be used. Quite soon the horse will, if he has halted reasonably well with his hocks under his hindquarters and not out behind, be able to trot from the halt. Riders must understand that if the horse is leaning on the hand, or is on the forehand, he will be unlikely to get from halt to trot satisfactorily.

In fact, following collection and the introduction of piaffe which some horses can begin quite early, the gathering of the hind legs under the horse can be very helpful in improving the transition from halt to trot.

How much obedience to expect and how to achieve it

A criterion in tests is that the horse must show his ability and acceptance to respond to an aid at a given marker.

At Novice level the horse is allowed to take his time, once the aid is given, to respond to the request although he must begin to respond as soon as he feels the cues. So a rider wishing to make a downward transition at B, must ask his horse before B, and allow the speed to reduce gradually. This would be allowed, but the rider must make sure that once his aid is given the horse responds, if not he will be reprimanded by the schooling whip, or by constant repetition until the aid is answered satisfactorily.

Gathering of the hind legs or the start of piaffe

From quite an early stage it can be very advantageous to start to teach the horse the meaning of the short steps on the spot.

Firstly, shorten the steps in walk by using half halts and then activating the hind legs in order to teach the hocks to flex and work under the body. The horse must be kept very calm and straight, the rider maintaining a very careful contact, not releasing too much but allowing the horse to move slightly forward. He should not restrict or hang on to the head but must concentrate on a close contact with the legs which may 'tap' for the required rhythm, and maintain an even steady contact with the head. If the horse swings about, becomes excessively excited, or above the bit, the exercise must be abandoned until he is in a more relaxed state of mind.

The rider will feel the horse become more active as the impulsion lifts the horse. There will be a feeling of bounce where there was flatness. A helper may be needed to obtain this for the rider to start with, by using the long whip just above the hocks to make the horse pick his legs up and come into the required rhythm.

Having started the exercise from walk in order to keep the horse calm and to keep the strides short enough, the gait will then gradually change until it becomes trot. When a few strides in a good rhythm have been achieved, the horse may then come back into walk, and if he has become tense or excited, must be made calm again.

During training, whenever the rider feels that he needs to bring the hind legs more under the body, or he needs greater activity, he may try bringing the horse to walk and asking the horse to work for a short time in this exercise.

Lengthening the trot

At Novice stage the horse is only required to show a few strides of lengthened trot and, in fact, he can probably only remain in balance for a few strides. This must always be born in mind, because as soon as the rider asks for length the horse will fall onto the forehand almost at once.

Balance must be the chief objective of the rider. In order to achieve it, the horse must first of all be straight and able to maintain a steady rhythm on the bit. The horse should also have been taught to shorten his stride and to maintain this 'short' trot carrying himself. This enables the hindquarters to come under the body, and until he can do this, he will not be able to lengthen correctly.

The rider should ask for the lengthening by closing the legs and holding the horse between them. If the legs alter in pressure or one becomes heavier than the other the horse may become crooked causing unevenness of stride. The rein contact must also be even and steady. Impulsion coming through from the hindquarters into the bridle will give the rider a firm feel with the hands. The feel should be elastic and not solid, because the horse's balance must not be such that he needs to lean on the rider's hands.

The stride required is longer with more lift to it, taking the horse over the ground in the same rhythm. Any sign of the strides quickening should instantly be checked as that is a sign of a lack of balance and correct lengthening will not be achieved unless there is good control and engagement of the hindquarters.

Beginning the counter canter

We teach this movement to test the horse's obedience to the aids, and improve the balance of the canter.

Counter canter in laymen's terms, is the canter 'on the wrong leg on purpose', and may seem very strange and awkward for the horse and rider at first.

If the balance is not carefully arranged by the rider, the horse will naturally change legs or become disunited, an even more uncomfortable feel.

To organise the balance so that the horse feels no necessity to change leg, the rider must ensure that his position is correct, i.e. the inside leg held at the girth for the bend and forward drive, and the outside leg behind the girth to prevent the hindquarters swinging and to help achieve spinal flexion. The lateral head flexion must be held to the leading leg, with support and control of the gait in the outside hand.

To begin with the rider may try a shallow loop along the side of the school, or arena, coming in from the track about

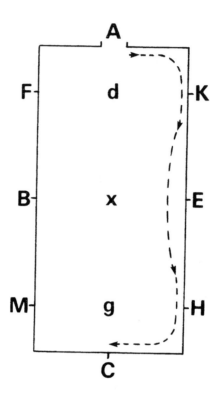

Fig. 9 Riding a shallow loop

1 m and returning very smoothly with little obvious change of direction (see Fig. 9).

The rider must sit on the inside seat bone throughout the loop because any change of weight may cause the horse to change leg.

If the deviation from the straight line is slight the horse will hardly notice any difference and the introduction to the exercise will be achieved.

Subsequently, deeper loops may be asked for, and

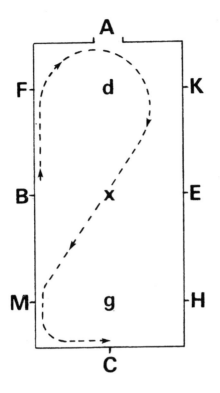

Fig. 10 Increasing the size of loop

changes of rein, arriving at the side of the school a stride or two early in order to ask for some counter canter (see Fig. 10).

Later in the horse's training, when he is more collected and supple, more difficult exercises incorporating some counter canter can be introduced.

Eventually the horse will be able to change direction easily remaining on the same leg whenever the rider wishes, without in any way becoming unbalanced.

Riding with one hand – 'Giving' the rein

It is occasionally required in the tests for the rider to ride for a few moments with one hand only, the other being held straight down by his side, though not held stiffly.

The rider must be able to control the horse, keep him straight and not interfere with the rhythm of the stride. This means that as he puts the reins into one hand (the outside hand unless otherwise stated) he must do so very carefully so that the contact is not suddenly altered in the horse's mouth. If the rider has taught the horse good acceptance of the bit, the smallest change of tension in his mouth will make him think he is to change direction, gait or speed. Most novice riders automatically take more pressure on the outside rein so they may need to alter the position of the one hand slightly to keep the tension equal. They must find this out for themselves which, being aware of the problem, they should be able to do.

When the reins are taken in both hands once more, the horse may change his head carriage so, again, care must be taken.

There is also a useful exercise called 'giving and retaking the reins'. This is used a lot in the training by the experienced rider, it tests the balance and ability of the horse to carry himself and also serves the purpose of relaxing and softening the neck muscles.

The rider has to actually break the contact with the horse's mouth with one or both hands for a few strides. He must not suddenly shoot his hands forward, but should gradually slide them forward on either side of the neck, not up the crest but forward towards the mouth. Then after a few strides the rider must regain contact without altering the horse's head carriage or causing any jerk on the bit.

The horse may follow the bit when the rein is given, so long as he does not snatch, and should stretch his neck a little, remaining in the same rhythmic stride, staying straight and not diving onto the forehand.

Evasions such as tilting the head, opening the mouth etc., can only be overcome if the horse is made to accept the bit by correct use of the aids.

Improving the transitions

More precision will now be asked for and the horse must be obedient enough, and physically able, to come or go from one gait to another within a few strides.

Instead of the rider taking his time and using the gaits progressively, he must demand directness, trot to halt and from halt, canter from walk and so on.

Although some transitions at this level may still be progressive, the rider should move up the ladder and start trying to achieve what will be needed for the next stage.

To improve the upward transitions, the rider must make sure that the horse is on the aids, that he is awake, listening and has sufficient impulsion to respond at once when the forward aid is given. The schooling whip may be used to achieve the necessary degree of preparation so that the horse is 'waiting to go', although he must in no way be tense or apprehensive.

Naturally forward-going horses are easier than lazy ones. They are usually half way ready themselves, but careful preparation must still be employed.

Lazy horses must be woken up to the aids so that they are mentally alert and sometimes this takes quite a long time. Resentment to being made to work harder and respond quickly may show itself in tail swishing, kicking to the leg aids, or even plain napping, all of which must be dealt with firmly and quickly so that the horse does not think he can get away with anything.

The schooling whip has to be used and the horse must respect it. Unfortunately he will only do that if he knows it can hurt him and sometimes it is necessary to be very strong minded and keep using the whip until the horse will listen and will ultimately answer to a small tap.

49

The downward transitions should now begin to show a small degree of collection prior to the alteration of the gait. If the shortening has been effective, the horse will be able to gather himself up from the increased aids of the rider and will then come into the new gait in a much more balanced and controlled way, thus being able to keep a steadier head carriage and rhythm.

If the shortening in canter is used just before the transition to the trot, there will be much less falling onto the forehand and the first few strides of the trot will then be better as a result.

At this standard, when making a transition from medium to working trot or canter, it would be acceptable for the horse to take a few strides to achieve the alteration. In order to obtain accuracy the rider should aim at decreasing the speed of the gait and tempo not more than four strides before the marker and achieving the transition as his leg reaches the marker.

If there is resistance in the mouth, or the hindquarters swing, they should be corrected by taking longer over the transition and the horse be given more time to find his balance.

To achieve enough difference between the working and medium gaits it is necessary to perform the transitions with as much definition as possible to show where the movement starts and finishes.

The direct transitions from walk to canter and from halt to trot must be done with tact, the rider feeling that the horse is awake and is ready to go forward but waiting until the aid is given.

If the rider is too strong with the hand especially at halt, the horse may feel restricted and he will be panicky thinking he is not going to be allowed to go forward. He may rear or just become unsettled, hence the rider must be careful. When making the transition to canter, the rider must ensure that the walk is straight and the canter position obtained before the aid is given. The rider must always make sure that the 'engine' or hindquarters of the horse are started up and begin the movement, and that he does not take himself forward with the front legs first.

The rider

Although a rider would not begin to try to train a horse unless he had the basic idea of the correct position and the influence the aids have over the horse, it is necessary for the rider to constantly check his position in the saddle and maintain it during the changes of gait.

The seat has the greatest influence over the horse. Relaxed seat muscles allow the rider to sit deep in the saddle and, if the rider's back is straight, directs the weight downwards through the seat bones not tipping the body forward or backward. The loins must be supple in order to absorb the movement of the horse, and the balance must be such that grip by the thighs is unnecessary except to a small degree.

The inside of the thighs must be flat against the saddle and the knee relaxed so that the lower part of the leg may rest against the horse with the toe forward. The ankle must also be supple to prevent any tension on the stirrup or unnecessary movement.

The arms should be held close to the rider's body and as naturally as possible with no tension of the joints, i.e. shoulder, elbow, wrist. The head should be held up looking between the horse's ears.

In walk the rider should follow the motion with the seat, and not 'shovel' the horse along by jerking as seen on some occasions. This causes tension in the horse's back and often hurries the steps.

In rising trot, the rider should leave the saddle as little as possible, rising and sitting in the same place each time in such a way that the lower leg does not swing, and the hands do not jerk in their contact. The seat may be brought forward a little with each rise in order to help this.

In sitting trot the rider must not bump on the saddle but

sit as still as possible keeping his legs round the horse and a light steady contact with his hands. If the arms are stiff, the contact will be at fault.

In canter the body must not swing or lean forward thus putting weight on the forehand.

The rider must at all times try to maintain his balance in order to help the horse, especially in the transitions.

Whilst not forgetting his position, the rider must remember that only he knows where he wants to go and at what gait, and it is his duty to prepare his horse in plenty of time for what is coming and to have the horse balanced in such a way that both can carry out the movement in harmony.

BHS Novice Test No 12

BEFORE A

Before the test starts I make sure that I have arrived at the arena in time to trot round the outside showing my horse the markers, the white boards, the judge's car and any other hazards which might be apparent, such as cows behind a hedge, umbrellas, dogs and so on.

I try to get the horse into a steady working trot which is the gait I have to enter in. If I have an assistant on the ground I may ask him if the trot looks steady and whether or not the outline is all right.

I usually go round on the stiff side to make sure that I am getting a flexion to that hand.

If I am near A when the bell goes I may go round the arena once more, or make a circle before entering because any hasty change of direction will upset my trot. If there is room I like to get well away from A, so that I can be straight for about ten yards before entering the arena.

The Entry

As soon as I have entered at A, I look at E and B to see where X is as I need to know long before I get there exactly where to stop. I also keep C between the horse's ears, and all the way I am concentrating on the mouth on the stiff side because when I stop I know the horse may resist on that side. If he does resist he will veer into that rein which I must not allow.

The Halt

I must allow the horse to square up and stand absolutely still before the salute.

The Move Off

Before the move off I must think ahead to which way I have to turn at C, and feel the rein a little more on the stiffer side trying to make sure the head position does not change as I give the aids to go forward.

The Turn Right

Just before G, I must position the horse to turn right by asking for the flexion to that side, and look to see where I am going to touch the track before and after the corner.

The Working Trot

As I come out of the corner I straighten the horse and ride on a little down the long side, making sure I am straight and keeping up a good tempo. Just before the next corner I must steady a little and make sure I have enough flexion for the corner.

Serpentine

I sit as carefully as possible so as not to alter the stride or the balance and look round to see where to cross the centre line. I must keep right flexion until just before I cross the centre line and then change it to the left flexion, having already looked ahead to B, which is the next place I must touch the track. Before B, I must look left to see where I next cross the centre line and I must change flexion over the centre line, as before. I now look to C, where the serpentine finishes.

The Strike Off

At C, I prepare the horse for canter by bringing him a little more together and making sure I have flexion and enough impulsion so that when I give the aid at M, he will strike off accurately and on the correct leg.

The 20 m Circle Right

I do not straighten the horse now I am in canter, but keep the flexion all the time to the leading leg. Before I get to B, I am looking to the right to see where to cross the centre line in order to touch the track at E, cross the centre line again and return to B, making my circle as uniformly round as I possibly can.

The Canter B To E

After the circle I go round the track riding the corners as well as I can and trying to do three or four straight strides on the short side. I must not ride the ends of the school like a half circle.

I am very aware, on the long side, of trying to keep my horse straight and not allowing the hindquarters to come in.

When I reach E, I look ahead to see the line of my 15 m diameter half circle making sure it is not too wide.

The 15 m Half Circle

I like to return to the track between E and K, and ride a few strides on the track before the transition so that the horse is straight before and at the marker.

All the way across the short diagonal I am keeping the outside leg back to keep the horse on the leading leg, but not using it so hard that he will go on two tracks.

I must keep my weight to the leading leg and keep the flexion to the right all the way to K.

As soon as the transition has taken place, I steady the trot which may be a little unbalanced at that point after the canter, and then I ride the following corner, making sure I have a left flexion before I reach it.

Serpentine

At A, I rise and ride the serpentine similarly to the last one, changing diagonals each time on crossing the centre line.

The Left Canter Circle, etc

At C, I sit and prepare the left canter and strike off, riding the circle and the 15 m half circle, and return to the track with as much flexion to the left as I showed to the right, showing that my horse is equal on both reins.

The Lengthened Strides

At A, I go into rising trot and before the corner I give a couple of small half halts to steady the balance before turning onto the diagonal.

I immediately look across the diagonal to M, to make sure I am straight and if I am steady I then ask for the lengthened strides. I must return to the working trot with a transition before M marker. Before M, I flex left, and having arrived on the corner I half halt to prepare for the walk at C.

Walk At C

I try to make sure my transition at C is straight and as soon as the horse walks I let him go forward into medium walk.

The Long Rein Walk

After the corner I turn onto the diagonal looking at the F marker, riding straight and allowing the horse to stretch his head as far as he wants to, keeping a light contact.

I start taking the reins up before F, so that as soon as I have turned onto the track I can ask for trot at F.

Up The Centre Line

At once I look round to what is the D position on the centre line to see how I must turn and having got onto the line I straighten and ride for C. Just after X, I begin asking for the halt so that when I arrive at G, the horse is steady and able to stop. Halt.

Having saluted, I walk on and allow the horse to stretch, turning right and then heading straight for A. I may give him a pat if he has been good and if not I must hide my disappointment behind a composed expression!

Part 3

Elementary and Advanced Elementary Standard

JUDGES' REQUIREMENTS
The judges will expect to see all the requirements of the Novice level now more established with the horse showing a slightly more raised forehand as the result of a greater degree of activity and carrying power of the hindquarters.

The gaits have to show more variation with greater precision of the transitions.

Rider and horse must be able to perform the pattern of the movements accurately and without difficulty or resistance.

FAULTS WHICH LOSE THE MOST MARKS
Outline not improved from Novice level.

Hindquarters sluggish.

Forehand not becoming lighter.

Not enough difference between the working, medium, or extended gait variations.

Inaccurately ridden movements.

Resistance caused by lack of balance or non-acceptance of the hand.

Not enough spinal flexion or angle in the shoulder-in.

Ten-metre circles losing impulsion and balance.

Horse not 'carrying' himself.

Unlevelness in extension.

Any irregularity of steps in walk or trot.
Stiffness and/or hollowing of the back.

Impulsion and balance

The Novice horse should already have attained a good degree of balance, although his impulsion cannot be as great as the Elementary horse.

Now the balance will gradually be becoming more established and the impulsion must be relative, so a greater degree of activity is asked for.

The rider should be able to ask the horse to bring his hind legs further under the body as a result of the exercises he is doing. As the horse takes more weight from the forehand his appearance will change: his fairly long outline will now become more compact. The hindquarters must be more engaged and the neck higher and more arched. He should not go on the forehand but should be light in hand and able to go on smaller circles and make deeper corners and turns without leaning on his rider for support.

The rider must use a greater degree of the half halt, and more positioning of the shoulders before many of the exercises to obtain the balance and activity he needs. For example, before riding 10 m circles in trot, the horse must be capable of coming from the working trot to some active shorter steps, and he must give a very small shoulder-in position at the start of the circle. To achieve this the rider will ask for a checking of the speed for several strides before the circle and may have to do this two or three times until the horse responds. The strides should shorten but not flatten or become quicker in rhythm. The rider should still feel a lift of the stride with the horse remaining straight and no mouth resistance.

He should than ask for the position, with the outside rein on the horse's neck well supported by the outside leg, using the inside leg to keep up the energy and the inside rein lightly flexing and directing the horse onto the circle.

He must not pull the horse onto the circle by too much inside rein, but must guide him on with the outside rein on the neck. Only this way will he have control of the outside shoulder which is absolutely essential to obtaining a true curve on the circle.

Stiffness and hollowing the back

One problem, which undoubtedly prevents the horse from using himself properly, is when the outline, or the line from the ears to the tail, becomes concave instead of convex. The term used in tests is usually 'hollowing the back', or 'flattening the back'.

If the horse is easing his back away from the weight of the rider the result is that the horse comes above the bit, and the hind legs, instead of being under the body, are pushed out behind. He is, therefore, not only unable to co-operate with his rider, but may also suffer pain. The back is weaker when hollow and, with the weight of the rider, damage can occur to the muscles along the spine. Consequently the rider must start again with whatever exercise he was attempting, having first corrected the mouth and head carriage and brought the horse properly under control.

Hollowing the back so often happens as the result of too much impulsion not under control, lack of balance and/or incorrect acceptance of the aids.

A lot of stiffness can set in if the horse is perpetually above the bit and hollow backed. To correct this, the mouth must be remade (a job for an expert) and the whole shape of the horse corrected, those muscles which have become shortened now have to be stretched and great care must be taken to do it correctly.

If the mouth is made softer and the head and neck brought lower, then the back will begin to round again and the hindquarters will once more become engaged.

Remaking the mouth is a tricky job and requires a lot of knowledge and feel which is difficult to describe in writing.

But riders should recall the way that the horse is asked to accept the bit in the first place: by feel and ease, and by resisting evasions until the jaw relaxes.

With the spoilt mouth, the resistance is multiplied, sometimes many times, and strength may have to be used to break it down. 'Strength' does not mean more and more force, but a stubborn persistance on the rider's part to keep the contact until the horse gives in. Only if this is achieved will any true acceptance ever be present.

The rider must have intense concentration and the ability to ease the instant he feels some relaxation on the horse's part. The hand immediately becomes stronger again if the horse's head goes up.

A pat on the neck is an encouragement to the horse if he is giving to the hand. He will learn what is wanted more quickly with some reward, but the reins must be put very carefully into one hand so that the contact is not altered or the whole feeling is lost!

Stiffness, which may develop as a result of resistance, must be corrected as soon as possible.

Young horses soon become one-sided and most seem to have a stiffer side, but this is probably due to their riders being right- or left-handed.

Riders must constantly be aware of any stiffness developing. They may feel it in the mouth when one side may become 'dead', and they will be unable to take a flexion to that hand. They may feel it with the leg as the horse lies against the leg on circles, turns, etc., instead of yielding to it.

The best exercise for improving flexion and suppleness, or for correcting stiffness, is the shoulder-in. By Elementary standard the horse should be able to maintain the correct angle (he must be on three tracks) for the length of the long side (40 m) of the school without difficulty. The outside rein controls the position and speed, and the inside leg on the girth must push the horse forwards making the horse bring the inside hind leg under the body. If the inside hind leg does not work enough, much of the purpose of the exercise is lost.

Once the horse is responding to the leg aid, the rider should catch the sideways movement with his outside rein to control the forehand. He must use the rein against the neck, not allowing the outside shoulder to escape, and go back to the track. He also has to be able to regulate the speed. The outside rein may need to be taken away from the neck to return the horse to the track if the angle is becoming too sharp, or it may need to be positioned on the neck to bring the outside shoulder in a little more.

The outside leg is used to stop the horse taking his whole body out onto the track as the inside leg is applied. The hindquarters have to be slightly curled round the rider's inside leg, so the horse must respond to the use of the outside leg behind the girth. If he takes no notice initially, the schooling whip may be used in the outside hand so long as the horse is responding to the use of the rider's inside leg. The inside rein should have a very light tension, only being there to keep a slight flexion to the inside and help maintain the angle. On no account should the rider try to push the horse sideways with the inside rein against the neck because this will only bend the neck too much, the outside shoulder will escape and the correct influence of the rider's inside leg to outside hand will be lost resulting in an incorrect shoulder-in.

When the horse can perform a correct shoulder-in at walk, and in a short trot (as near to collection as possible at this level of training) then the rider can be sure of being able to correct stiffness which will occur during training. I say 'will', because inevitably difficulties arise when trying to teach the horse some new exercise, and any difficulty can cause resistance and stiffness.

Improving shoulder-in

As mentioned earlier, the shoulder-in is an exercise vital to the entire training of the horse. Achieving a correct shoulder-in is problematical for both horse and rider, especially if both are novices.

Throughout training the rider must have the ability to control and position the horse's shoulders, in order to prepare for an exercise, straighten the horse, or place the forehand in such a position that the horse can more easily perform an exercise.

To begin with the rider will attempt to teach the horse shoulder-in in walk, to give him the idea of the position, and the aids. He may start on a 10 m circle making the horse flex/curve round his inside leg by drawing the outside leg back behind the girth, and by making sure that the horse will flex and 'give', to the inside hand. The outside rein must ensure that not only the neck is flexed, but the spinal flexion is throughout the whole length of the horse.

If he is satisfied that the horse is paying attention to each hand and leg, he may then leave the circle and proceed up the long side of the school, immediately riding the front feet in from the track as though to begin the circle. Keeping the curve, he then must push the horse away from the inside leg so that the hind feet remain on the track, and the front feet remain just off the track.

As soon as the inside leg is applied the rider must support the horse at once with his outside hand to control the position and speed, which must be kept slow in the early stages.

The driving inside leg must be reinforced by the schooling whip if needed. The outside leg must maintain the curve and control the hindquarters, the hands must allow the horse to move forward a little, keep the horse at the correct angle and prevent him merely walking off onto a circle.

Only a few steps should be asked for at first, and then the horse may be taken onto a 20 m circle maintaining the spinal curvature. Gradually the number of steps must increase until the rider can go some distance up the long side keeping the angle.

To begin with, the amount of angle should bring the horse

onto three tracks or less (see Fig. 5) but this increases as training progresses and so does the amount of spinal flexion (see Fig. 11).

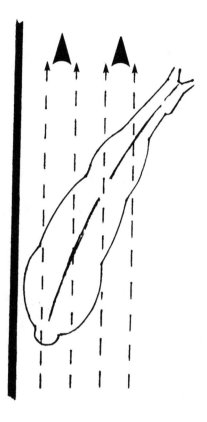

Fig. 11 Increased angle and spinal flexion

When the horse has understood the position and aids at walk, the rider may then consider the trot, but first the horse must be able to maintain a short trot in balance, approaching collection because he will not be able to hold the angle required if the strides are long.

The rider must also be able to effect a small half halt used during the shoulder-in in order to keep the horse at a speed at which he can easily hold the required angle.

The rider must make sure that he does not bend the horse's neck round, lose the outside shoulder, make the angle too great for the stage of the training, allow the hindquarters to fall out, or allow the horse to 'run away' from the inside leg.

When all these details have been sorted out and resistances overcome, the rider will discover a much more satisfactory state of control which will have been well worth the effort.

Commencing gait variations

The judges requirements for this standard state that the lengthening and shortening of the strides is now needed and the rider will need to understand how to proceed with this, without risking spoiling the rhythmic steady steps he has established.

WALK SHORTENING
Although no collected walk is asked for, the horse must begin to learn to shorten in the walk, so that he is ready for the next stage, and to improve his obedience and acceptance of being 'brought more together', by the increased aids of the rider.

The rider must sit and apply his aids evenly so that straightness can be maintained. The horse will almost certainly resist any extra pressure on his mouth, and the hindquarters will surely swing to evade the legs. The rider should first slow down to shorten the stride, i.e. the hind feet not tracking over the imprint of the forefeet.

The rider must make sure the horse remains straight, and that he still has even acceptance to the hand. If the horse should resist by opening his mouth, crossing his jaw or coming above the bit, the short steps should be maintained until the horse has yielded to the hands. If the mouth is soft and the horse straight, the rider should ask for activity of the hind legs. It will be no good having activity if there is resistance in the mouth, but equally it will be useless to have a soft mouth and a horse which is not going forward. The schooling whip may be employed to bring about the activity, which is the energy provided by the hind legs in order to push the horse forward.

Only a few steps at a time should be asked for, until the horse learns to hold the steps himself without any force on the part of the rider. To ask for more would be too difficult and could cause more resistance.

TROT SHORTENING

A similar procedure is applied in the trot, the horse being asked to carry himself for a few short steps at a time, without leaning on the rider's hands.

The rider's feel is critically important now as the technique is more difficult in trot, the balance being lost easily and resistance and unlevel steps can all too easily become a habit.

The rider must concentrate on the balance, using tiny half halts to control the impulsion and pressure on the bit, and using his legs evenly and closely to the horse's sides keeping him moving forward smoothly, but not impulsively. The horse may lurch forward suddenly, or suddenly drop into walk. It is the rider's job to control this and teach him that he can trot very slowly with short steps without difficulty.

Should any unlevelness occur, it may be necessary to return to walk and start again making sure that no stiffness or hardness of the mouth recurs.

A long-striding horse will often find it difficult to shorten and increase the tempo. As the rider slows him down he still takes long steps and sometimes becomes too elevated or lifts his front legs too high. The rider must seek for short quicker steps from him, encouraging this to happen by starting from walk and asking for piaffe-like steps, almost on the spot. If the horse should try to passage, and have too much elevation, he must be returned to walk and the aid repeated until he gives what is wanted. If the mouth is soft and the back round, he will learn to trot with shortened steps.

CANTER SHORTENING

In canter, the shortening must be done without any hollowing of the horse's back. If this happens, as a result of him coming above the bit, his back muscles may become damaged which would be very detrimental to his future training. He must only perform a slower canter with the mouth soft and the back round, and without losing the three-time beat of the steps. He must be kept straight and not allowed to put his hindquarters in. The rider must now be capable of using a small shoulder-in position to effect the straightening. The hindquarters must never be pushed out. The rider should try to hold the hindquarters evenly with his legs and then bring the forehand in slightly so that it comes in line with the hindquarters. Then, by stronger use of the inside leg into the outside rein the rider will gain more control and be able to hold the horse straight.

The rider should use working to short canter and return to the working canter until the horse will make the change easily from one to the other.

Once the horse has learnt to accept the rider's aids for shortening the strides, he will be more obedient and physically able to carry himself more easily. Only then will he be able to start some lengthening as the result of the hindquarters being brought under the body.

It is usually a mistake to allow the horse to lengthen the strides until the hind legs are working under him, if they are not, when the horse is asked to go more forward, he will push off with his hind legs behind, instead of under, his body. This causes lack of balance and falling on the forehand, lack of extension and later, when more lengthening is required, the hind legs become wide behind in their efforts to propel the horse on to a longer stride.

WALK LENGTHENING

Lengthening in the walk is usually achieved best after a period of trot work when the horse has been using all his muscles quite energetically and is pleased to walk and stretch. It can also be encouraged and improved by the use of the schooling whip and by making the horse go more forward.

TROT LENGTHENING

Lengthening of the trot is offered by the horse himself when his hind legs are under his body, his balance is steady, and there is sufficient impulsion.

He will have arrived at this point as a result of acceptance of light aids, good balance and activity, and the ability to push himself forward from the shortened steps.

The rider will only need to squeeze a little with his legs and hold the forehand steady to find that the horse will start to lengthen his strides. This will happen, if the preparation has been correct, unless the horse is very short striding naturally. This can be a problem as any urging on the part of the rider may result in quickening from the horse instead of lengthening.

If the horse 'runs' faster when the aids are given, he must immediately be slowed down, the rhythm corrected and the whole operation tried again.

A horse with a short stride in trot is a handicap to an aspiring dressage rider and only with careful and clever riding can this be improved. The horse must not, whatever happens, be allowed to go on the forehand and this must be foremost in the rider's mind. The short striding horse must learn to lift his shoulders to make a better-length stride, and if there is any weight on the forehand, he cannot do this.

The long-striding horse can usually lengthen naturally or, at any rate, finds it easier than one with a short quick stride.

However, the rider must beware of allowing the horse with natural length to use it in his own way, which may be a flamboyant flinging about of the forelegs which will not necessarily be under control. It is also easy to imagine that the horse is lengthening the stride if his shoulders lift naturally, allowing freedom of the forelegs. With this sort of horse it is very important to check that the hind legs are under the body and not left behind, that the hocks are flexing and that the horse's mouth and back are correct.

An ideal action in trot is one which is slightly rounded in front and has a good natural flexion of the hocks.

CANTER LENGTHENING

Lengthening the canter should be asked for when the balance of the working canter is good and when the horse has learned to come under more control by the increased aids of the rider used to obtain shortening and straightening.

He must then go onto a longer stride in the same rhythm with a longer moment of suspension in between each stride. It will be incorrect, therefore, if he should set off almost at gallop because the canter will be flat and there will not be any suspension between the strides.

The rider must drive the horse more forward, with his legs still and close to the horse's sides, using the schooling whip as an aid if necessary. He must not allow any dropping onto the forehand but must hold the balance level with seat and hand. The horse should bring his hind legs further under him which will push him forward and upward a little, creating the moment of suspension, keeping his neck arched, his forehand light, and his mouth soft. The rider must expect more power in his hands, but no leaning or pulling.

If the horse twists his head, puts his hindquarters in, or will not return sensibly to the working canter after the lengthening, the rider must reduce the amount of length asked for and correct the faults.

Improving the outline

The increased activity and carrying power of the hindquarters (engagement) are the key factors to the improvement of the outline and the lightening of the forehand.

At Elementary level the horse is still in a transitional stage with regard to the control he has over himself and his balance, and his ability to remain steady. The rider must keep a picture in his mind of the ultimate carriage expected of the Advanced horse, so that he can work towards this, stage by stage.

The greater engagement of the hindquarters is possible when there is a more complete acceptance of the rider's hand. (Some resistance to new aids and/or movements is to be expected but it should lessen all the time.)

This acceptance means that any increased activity created by the rider is able to travel through the horse, meeting no resistance, and will take the horse forward. Therefore, to engage the hindquarters the rider will:

1. Ask for more activity and impulsion from the hind legs. They must work *under* the horse *not* out behind him.
2. By using half halts the rider will gradually take weight off the forehand and ask the hind legs to carry more of the horse's weight.

If the hind legs are under the horse he will be able to comply. If not, he will try to push himself forward, but the thrust will be more difficult for him and he may go wide behind and also flatten his back. This elongated position will be a hindrance to his further development and his ability to be truly collected.

The outline of the Elementary horse should be similar to the Novice horse, but with the hindquarters more under the body, the forehand a little higher, the neck more arched, and the head nearer to the vertical position.

The horse must be able to shorten and collect himself with the outline essentially the same, but a little rounder in shape, and certainly no shortening of the neck or forehand only.

There should be a little more lift of the shoulders as the forehand lightens with some small increase in the moments of suspension in trot and canter.

Preparation and positioning

FURTHER HALF HALTS

The two exercises which are the most useful in preparing for a movement are the half halt and the shoulder-in.

Riders do not incorporate these valuable aids to the balance and control nearly enough, particularly at the lower stages. The degree of both the half halt and the shoulder-in prior to beginning a movement may be very small and, at this stage, may be recognised as a slight check in the speed in place of a real half halt, and a small positioning of the forehand rather than a shoulder-in.

The horse is, for a moment, asked to come more together, be balanced, and ready to go where required.

PREPARATION

With regard to the preparation, the rider must appreciate the length of time it takes the horse to comprehend the aid he is given by the rider and then put his understanding into operation. The rider must, therefore, think clearly, well ahead, what his intention is, so that by the time he arrives at the appointed place, the horse is actually ready to obey.

Some of the exercises need to have moments of collection, e.g. where there is a corner followed by a turn at A, or a 10 m circle in working trot. Before the turn or circle the rider will need to steady the horse, even shorten the stride fractionally for a moment to ensure that the strides are not too long causing loss of balance and difficulty.

Sometimes it is necessary to give two or three steadying aids to bring the impulsion under control. This is so particularly with the naturally impulsive horse. Lazy horses need half halts too but the rider has to ride these with a stronger seat and leg, not necessary with the excitable horse.

HALF HALTS FOR ELEMENTARY WORK

With impulsive horses the half halt is generally used to reduce impulsion and steady the gait. The rider must not think that there is no need to use his legs! It is very important to keep the horse quite firmly between the calves of the legs in order to keep him forward to the hand, and to control the hindquarters and keep him straight. Then the hands must ask the horse to steady the gait, having first used the legs so that he does not escape backwards, swing the hindquarters or lose his activity. The rider may need to use this aid repeatedly until the impulsion is held in the hindquarters and is not surging into the hands too much, causing leaning and resistance.

A lazy horse is given the same aids as an impulsive one, but the reaction is different. Although he may steady the gait he will almost certainly lose too much impulsion so that the rider must increase the use of the legs and seat and enforce them with the schooling whip. If this makes the horse go forward into the hand too much, the aid has to be repeated again until the balance is correct and the horse becomes light in hand.

POSITIONING
This can be explained by the rider thinking of shoulder-in, although it is the control over the horse's shoulders he is seeking and not actually a full shoulder-in position.

Before the turns, circles and corners, the rider should endeavour to concentrate on both of the horse's shoulders. The horse must not lie on the inside shoulder, nor must the outside shoulder escape.

If the horse has already been taught the shoulder-in exercise, he will allow the rider to position him by flexing the spine under the saddle, not in the neck, thus keeping the forehand fairly straight, but with the forelegs fractionally and momentarily in from the track. As soon as the movement is commenced the positioning may be dropped but not the control of the shoulders.

From the positioning, the rider gains control of the forehand and, by the increased use of his inside leg, brings the horse's inside hind leg further under the body, thereby facilitating better balance. The rider's aim is to prepare and position all in one go.

71

The outside rein will be controlling the speed and the outside shoulder. The inside rein is directive in bringing the inside foreleg into position but not allowing him to step to the side.

The outside leg will be controlling any outward swing of the hindquarters and, in fact, curving the horse round the inside leg. The inside leg will be keeping up the impulsion, creating spinal flexion, and at the same time both legs keep the horse into the bridle.

The horse must be able to change position for a change of direction, eventually, quite quickly, so it is important to build a sound basis at this stage and to constantly check the balance which will enable the horse to answer the aids.

Resistances (temperaments)

During the training the rider will find, inevitably, that things will go wrong. His horse will for some reason or another develop some tiresome evasion, which if handled immediately and correctly need never take hold and become a real problem. The rider should not despair if one of the following difficulties occur as it happens to the best riders, but if he cannot overcome it by himself, he should seek help from someone more experienced.

Difficulties very often occur due to the different temperaments horse have.

Excitable types quite often grind their teeth, open their mouths or tilt their heads because the impulsion is not, really under control and both horse and rider are struggling.

Lazy horses will frequently swish their tails or nap because they do not want to go forwards.

It is important for the rider to understand what temperament he is dealing with so that he can work out the best way of handling the situation.

TILTING THE HEAD

A common evasion which can be exceedingly irritating is when the head is slanted with the ears tipping one way and the nose the other. Usually it happens because the horse is stiff on one side and when asked to bend that way he evades the issue by tilting his head.

A horse whose muscles are stiffer on the left side will tilt his nose to the left thus not giving a true flexion. On the right rein, because he finds it easier, the tilt may be less apparent but, if asked to flex more, the tilt to the left will still be there.

Therefore, whenever there is difficulty with keeping the head straight, the rider must first correct the mouth, making sure that the acceptance is even. To do this he will need to keep his left rein quite steady (if the nose is tilting left) and draw on the right rein to bring the nose to the right and the head straight.

Once the head is straight he must then work on the lateral flexion making sure that the horse is yielding to the leg and that he can create spinal flexion with his inside leg rather than the rein.

A true curve must be achieved, with no evasions of this kind if there is to be any real future for the horse in dressage, so it is important to get this fault put right.

OPENING THE MOUTH

The most common of the bit evasions. The horse will open his mouth to relieve himself of the correct or incorrect pressure of the bit thereby avoiding the acceptance.

Many other difficulties occur as a result of this evasion such as the tongue coming over the bit, or coming out of the side of the mouth. Also the horse can tilt his head more easily, lean on the bit, or, in fact, put his head where he likes because the rider has little control.

The easiest prevention is for the horse to wear a drop noseband instead of a cavesson from the beginning of his training. If fitted correctly it causes no discomfort and helps to keep the mouth closed and, therefore, the bit in the right place.

It is far more uncomfortable for the horse if, when he opens his mouth, the bit ring goes into the sides of his mouth which can happen with a cavesson noseband. Also, if he learns to put his tongue over the bit, it can be difficult to correct and will recur in times of stress. It is much easier to adopt the old adage, 'prevention is better than cure'.

It is quite difficult enough to teach the horse to accept the bit, without having any extra problems to cope with!

GRINDING THE TEETH

Anxiety and tension sometimes causes teeth grinding or chattering, and if either become a habit, can be extremely difficult or impossible to eradicate.

If the rider understands the cause, he must do his best to avoid getting the horse into a state, mentally and physically, when teaching him a new exercise.

Given time most horses can learn almost anything but they must be calm to be receptive. It is up to the rider to relax the horse and then, by quiet repetition, get what he wants.

Consistent aids are very important to the horse's understanding so the rider must know clearly in his own mind what and how he is asking for something and then use his aids for each different exercise, exactly in the same way each time.

Most riders develop their own 'buttons' for riding their horse and each rider will like a different amount of weight in the hand, pressure with the leg, and so on.

As long as the horse knows what is coming and is prepared in plenty of time, he will obey. If muddle occurs and the horse becomes het up and starts to grind his teeth, the rider should stop what he is doing, try something easier which the horse can do calmly, or go back and check on the acceptance of the bit and then, by devious means if necessary, return to the exercise causing the problem.

When I say devious means, riders must use their ingenuity when training to gain their particular horse's confidence and attention, and there can be no set rules laid down for the way each rider builds the relationship with his horse.

OVERBENDING

Generally speaking this is an evasion, the horse bending too much at the poll, with the head coming behind the vertical. The horse is able to avoid taking the pressure of the bit and can then avoid the proper contact of the rider's hands. Very often this evasion is caused by the unsympathetic or heavy hands of the rider which will have caused the horse pain and so he finds a way out. Riders are unsympathetic mainly for two reasons. They may not have the knowledge to place the horse correctly on the bit, and so lack the finesse of when to feel and ease, or, they may have an insecure seat which will result in holding themselves in balance by the reins.

Whatever the reason, if the horse is becoming overbent, the rider should first look to his own ability, or lack of it, before blaming the horse. The horse may overbend sometimes owing to the difficulty of a new exercise but if the rider is sensitive to the correct head carriage he will recognise this quickly and correct it.

If the horse is overbent he will almost certainly be slightly on the forehand and so the balance is the first thing to try to improve. By using steadying aids the rider must reduce the speed, and make the horse carry himself more on the hindquarters and bring the hind legs under the body making the balance more level. The rider should take an even contact, not loosening it under any circumstance (taking up the slack of the rein if necessary) and then push the horse on to the bit with the legs.

In so doing he should not increase the tempo to start with, but should aim to build some energy in the hindquarters which, if successful, will go through to the bit making the horse desire to stretch towards the bit instead of away from it.

Gradually the length of the stride may then be increased, with the rider being careful to keep enough impulsion but not too much, and an even light contact with the mouth.

Overbending, like other problems, can become difficult to correct if left too long and is best dealt with as soon as the rider is aware of it happening.

TAIL SWISHING
A tiresome habit which is generally due to a non-acceptance of the leg aids. The horse does not like the pressure, or the leg being drawn back, or being forced to go forwards when he does not feel like it.

If persistent, it can lose quite a lot of marks in a test because it shows the horse's reluctance to co-operate. An occasional swish is not penalised much, if at all, as long as the dock is not set adamantly.

The schooling whip must be used to obtain the acceptance of the leg because if the obedience is not absolute, some resistance will occur, if not at the time, later in the training when the work becomes more difficult.

Horses who swish their tails are quite often nappy and this is absolutely no good if the horse is to progress.

In the beginning the young horse must accept the pressure of the rider's legs on his side, without resentment, and also accept a tap with the schooling whip, without kicking at it. If there is resistance to the leg and/or the whip, a firm line must be taken because the horse must be in no doubt that when one or the other is applied he must go forward.

CROSSING THE JAW
This fairly common evasion is seen when the horse wishes to disobey the rein aids; he may move his lower jaw from side to side to evade the pressure and to avoid the rider's request.

It is often seen on the centre line when coming to the halt, the horse will resist, usually to one side, in order to relieve his mouth on that side.

More even acceptance of the bit is needed and, possibly, better preparation by the rider as quite often there is a much too sudden application of the aids which the horse cannot obey because the impulsion has to be reduced first.

More circles

Many circles will be ridden during training. They are important to the development of the muscular system, and teach the horse to flex his spine to a greater or lesser degree and use his inside hind leg under the body.

Circles may be of various sizes beginning with 20 m diameter and reducing in size to the 6 m diameter volte (see Fig. 12). Larger circles require very little lateral flexion from the horse and riders must beware of bending the neck too much, preventing a true curvature throughout the length of the horse.

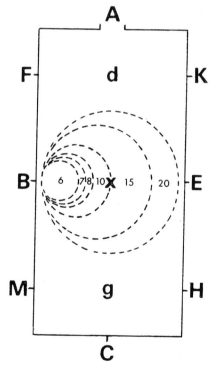

Fig. 12 Various circle sizes – numbers indicate diameter in metres

77

At all times the control must be in the rider's outside hand, i.e. control of the speed and direction, so that the outside hand determines the circle size, and not the inside. The rein should be used on the neck and the horse feeling this will come round onto the circle.

To make the aid clear to a young horse, the rider's inside hand may move away from the neck (to the inside): this is called an open rein. If the horse should fall onto his inside shoulder, better use of the outside rein and inside leg together should make the correction. The inside hand may place the rein against the neck for a few strides to assist with this correction.

As the circle size reduces, so the spinal flexion increases (see Fig. 12) but this must happen as a result of the leg aids: inside leg on the girth, outside behind the girth. The horse must curve his body round the inside leg. The neck flexion should increase with the body flexion so that the curve is true throughout the length of the horse.

HEAD FLEXIONS

Not only must the rider be able to create a true spinal flexion (see Fig. 13) he must also be able to take a head flexion to left or right at any time as a warning or preparatory aid, or to help to increase spinal flexion.

These head flexions occur at the point where the head joins the neck and, put simply, the poll and the lower jaw must yield if pressure is applied.

When a head flexion is requested the rider will take the inside rein firmly and ask the horse to turn the head, but not the neck. He must not step towards the flexion but must continue in a straight line. The horse will feel soft in the mouth on the flexed side and the straightness will be maintained by the rider's legs and the outside hand, controlling the speed and direction.

Arriving at a correct spinal flexion depends in particular on the balance and collection at the time, and whether the horse will accept leg and hand. The rider must think carefully about the arc of the circle he is following and look

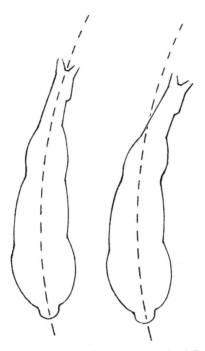

Fig. 13 Correct and incorrect spinal flexion

ahead to make sure he is riding the circle points correctly.

He must also pay attention to the way he is sitting because if there is any crookedness in the seat, shoulders or hands, the horse will not be able to carry out a true arc.

Developing counter canter

This exercise has already been mentioned briefly, but I think it worth reminding the reader that before beginning the counter canter the horse's balance and ability to collect himself, must be fairly well established.

The canter should have a definite moment of suspension, and the horse must be able to carry himself without leaning on the bit. He must be quite supple and obedient to the outside leg.

The easiest place to begin the exercise is on the long side of the arena or school, as the rider can ask for a small deviation from and to the track, with very little disturbance to the balance.

The rider should first aim at coming in gradually from the quarter marker and returning to the track by the quarter marker at the other end of the long side of the school, having come off the track only one or two feet (see Fig. 9). He must not suddenly change direction and he must keep the flexion to the leading leg. He must keep his own weight on the side of the leading leg, and he must keep his outside leg back to hold the hindquarters round his inside leg.

The horse must not speed up as he goes through the loop which he may try to do when he feels he is more firmly on the outside leg than usual. He must not return to the track on two tracks (sideways) which may happen if the rider does not make sure that the horse is straight, i.e. hind legs following the forelegs. He must not change legs in front and become disunited which may happen if the rider is careless and changes weight, or loses the correct flexion, or changes the direction too quickly.

A progression from this exercise is to try a shallow serpentine of three loops to either side of the centre line. At first the deviation must be very small so that the horse hardly notices any change of direction. The lateral head flexion to the leading leg must be maintained and the loops ridden evenly; that is to say, the same distance either side of the centre line. If the rider has no line to follow, if he keeps his eye on the C marker this should help him to judge the movement more accurately. At any rate the middle loop must be round X.

Riders may now like to improve the obedience to the canter aids and to develop the counter canter by doing strike offs round the school, sometimes on the true lead, and sometimes the counter lead.

At first it should only be attempted on the straight and the horse must be well positioned.

Do not confuse the horse by stopping each canter too

quickly. Otherwise he will very soon feel muddled as to which leg he is meant to be on, he must be allowed to canter the length of the long side at least, and quite soon anyway he should be asked to go round the first corner, increasing this until he will go round the end of the school and then the whole way round in counter canter.

Pirouettes in walk

Although pirouettes are not actually asked for in the Elementary tests, the horse should be taught to do them. Even at Novice level some riders will like to teach the horse to answer the pirouette aids and to come round, answering the hand and making the hindquarters move away from the outside leg. It not only helps the rider to gain more control, but he makes the horse work behind the saddle.

The rider should first consider what he is trying to do. He wants to draw the horse's forehand to the side, keeping a slight lateral head flexion to the direction he is going and, at the same time, prevent the horse's hindquarters swinging into his outside leg, which will be the natural reaction. He must take the inside rein a little away from the horse's neck to show him which way he is to go. The outside rein will come against the neck and will control the forward impulsion and the amount of neck bend.

The inside leg will maintain spinal curve and keep the horse forward to the bit, and the outside leg (all important) will come against the horse's side, behind the girth, and push him sideways and round. Any swinging of the hindquarters into the outside leg must be checked instantly with the schooling whip.

With a young horse it sometimes helps to use the whip on the outside shoulder to get him started but once he has the idea, this is not necessary.

The steps must be controlled, the horse coming round evenly and not making one large step and then several smaller ones. It must be so controlled that if the rider wishes, he may stop or go forwards at any time.

The hind legs must be mobile and very often it is necessary to start the turn, walk forward two steps, turn again and so on until a 180 degree turn is completed. This way the horse is kept up to the bit and the flexion may be corrected during the turn. The rider must beware of restricting the turn so that the horse feels that he cannot go forward which may cause him to run back or resist in other ways. The rider may keep the horse in the pirouette for more than 180 degrees during training in order to achieve the acceptance of his aids, or improve the activity of the hind legs but it is not required in the tests, and unless the rider is fairly experienced he may cause problems by doing this.

Leg yield

Leg yielding is seldom required in the arena and not at Elementary level.

However it is an exercise useful to the general training and is helpful to horse and rider in understanding and being obedient to the beginning of the lateral work.

Less experienced riders may find that it helps them to get the feel of the horse moving away from the leg and crossing behind, and both will find it easier than the half pass, at the start. There is a slight lateral head flexion away from the direction of movement.

Experienced riders may use leg yield at any time during training at any level, for a moment as a correction, or because some stiffness has developed which they wish to overcome.

The less knowledgable must be content to learn it as something preparatory to half pass, or for teaching the horse to increase his attention to the inside leg when being asked for spinal flexion.

When beginning the exercise the rider may start up the centre line and move the horse forwards and slightly sideways – at one and the same time – keeping him parallel to the long side. He should eventually arrive on the long side straight without the forehand, or the hindquarters, arriving first.

To start with, only a few steps should be asked for so he will only just leave the centre line and then, if he has answered the aids satisfactorily, he will be asked to go straight forward to the end of the school before turning right or left.

Later the rider may ask for a few steps sideways, then a few straight forward, then a few more sideways.

He should aim at starting at D, and finishing at M, to get the right amount of sideways movement.

The rider should ask the horse to move over by using the inside leg, (and whip if necessary, tapping behind the leg). When the horse swings his hindquarters over as he may do, the outside leg must catch them and send the horse forwards before the inside leg asks again.

The rein contact should be fairly even to keep the forehand straight. The hands guide the horse across in the direction he is going with a very slight curve in the direction away from the movement.

If the forehand leads and the hindquarters are not keeping up, the rider should stop and regain control over the whole length of the horse before trying again.

The horse should not be allowed to do the exercise if he is tilting his head or twisting his neck.

On the circle, the leg yield is slightly different as more curvature is used to the inside, and the horse pushed sideways round the circle, with the forehand in and the hind legs on the line of the circle. It is not the same as shoulder-in because, in the leg yield, the horse is pushed sideways to make him give to the inside leg, in a rather exaggerated way and this is only done for a few steps and then the correct spinal flexion must be resumed.

Some trainers prefer never to use leg yielding and will go straight to the half pass, which is an accepted classical movement.

Half pass

To teach the horse and/or rider to understand the half pass, it may help to begin in walk.

The first thing to achieve is to make the horse step sideways away from the outside leg, advancing forwards and sideways at the same time. A good place to ask is from the centre line to the long side as the rider can see whether he is keeping the horse parallel to the centre line and long side, and, if not, can make the necessary corrections. He should take the length of the school to achieve the half pass to the long side and, in the beginning, will probably only go a few steps sideways and then straight forwards.

At first it will not matter if there is slight flexion away from the direction in which the horse is travelling, although of course this will be a leg yield and not half pass.

Once the horse will respond to the use of the outside leg and will step away from it, the rider must begin to work on the correct head flexion. In fact, he must insist on a lateral flexion to the direction in which he is travelling before asking the hindquarters to come over. He should obtain the correct flexion on a 10 m diameter circle and go from the circle into the half pass without losing it. The forehand may precede the hindquarters slightly to start with but the hindquarters must be made to keep up and not trail behind if the movement is to be of value. If the hindquarters should come over more than the forehand, the horse must be taken straight forward, repositioned and then asked again. Riders find it difficult to control the forehand sufficiently and many will allow the horse to rush sideways onto the inside shoulder, e.g. if half passing to the left, the left shoulder. This will very quickly give a wrong bend as the horse cannot take the weight on the left inside shoulder without losing balance.

The rider must be very conscious of the control he has over the shoulders, and be able to lead the forehand over more, should the hindquarters begin to lead, or he should slow the forehand to allow the hindquarters to keep up if the horse is trying to go sideways too quickly.

The inside leg must be used to keep the correct flexion of the horse and to push him forwards to maintain impulsion and re-establish the spinal curvature if it is lost.

If the flexion is lost the rider must cease the sideways action of the aids until he has corrected the flexion through the horse, and then recommence the exercise.

Young horses find it difficult to flex the spine and go sideways at the same time, therefore very little flexion must be asked for and the rider must be patient. As the horse becomes more supple he will find it easier. The spinal flexion will be slightly increased with the degree of training of the horse.

When the horse has learned the exercise in walk, he may be asked to do it in trot, but he must be able to do a collected trot, i.e. short balanced steps, or there will be difficulty and resistance. The rider should ask for a few steps forward/sideways, then a few straight forward to regain the correct balance and flexion, then forward/sideways again.

The fore and hind legs must cross evenly, each step being the same width. It is a mistake to allow too big a step sideways to start with until the control of the inside shoulder is established.

When the horse has the idea of the half pass to the right, and to the left, he may be asked to do a small zig zag, a few steps in one direction and then a few in the other. It is almost certainly necessary to go back to walk until the horse understands the idea of the zig zag exercise and the aids.

Begin on the long side of the school coming round the corner with the correct bend and going immediately into half pass towards the centre line. After four or five forward/sideways steps, take the horse straight forward a moment, and then commence the second half pass back to the track. This may be built up so that there are two counter canter changes of hand up one long side of a 40 m arena.

At the moment of the change over from one half pass to the other, the straight forward step must be carried out with the outside hind leg, and the inside hind leg must immediately cross over in front and commence the next half pass, i.e. if the horse is in half pass right and the rider wishes to change to half pass left, he must make the horse take one step forward between the two half passes, making sure that it is the near hind which takes the forward step, and the off hind which crosses and begins the new half pass.

The rider must not allow any rushing from one to the other, and must be in control of both forehand and hind-quarters, ceasing the exercise if the horse is rushing. When the half pass in walk is under control, the horse may be asked to do it in collected trot, starting with a little impulsion and as the horse becomes responsive to the aids and learns to hold his balance the impulsion may be increased.

The rein-back

At about this time in the horse's training rein back should be started, although it is not required in a test until the Medium dressage test.

To start the exercise too soon can cause problems with the halt because the horse will, in anticipating going backwards, either fidget at halt or step back out of hand. If he is not sufficiently prepared, i.e. taught to accept the hand correctly, resistance will almost certainly occur which will cause a set jaw, stiffness, caused by the horse hollowing his back, and other faults, which will prevent him from stepping back under control. He may also injure muscles if the rider should force him back against his will or before he is ready. He should have developed some muscle along the spine and not be weak in the hindquarters.

The rider will ask for a square balanced halt with the hind legs under the body not out behind. He must achieve this by bringing the horse to the halt with his legs firmly putting the horse on to the bit, which the horse should accept with bent poll and relaxed jaw. If the halt is correct the rider may then ease the leg pressure to allow the horse to step back as he feels a little more on the mouth. At each step the hands must ease and feel again for the next step, in order that the steps are slow, deliberate and under control.

The rider's legs control the speed and length of the backward steps so he can allow them to be longer or shorter depending on his requirements at that moment. In the beginning the steps should be quite short, until the rider knows that he has the horse in his control. Later the steps should be of a similar length to those when moving forward.

As many horses find difficulty in reining-back under the rider, the rider may, at first help by leaning forward slightly to allow the spine of the horse to round which will help him to make the steps back and will prevent any hollowing of the back or dragging of the hind legs.

The horse must not be allowed to lower the neck, bear down on the hands and push himself back or try to reverse on the forehand. He must also remain straight between the rider's legs and answer the aid to go forward immediately it is given, using his hind legs under him to start the forward movement. Ideally the stride which finishes the rein-back should begin the next forward stride. As the legs move diagonally in rein-back, if the horse goes four steps, finishing with the near fore and off hind, the off hind should touch the ground and straight away come forward again to begin the forward walk.

When the horse is learning, it will be sufficient if he steps back one complete stride, straight and without resistance. Gradually, as he understands the aid, the rider may ask for more steps, but not more than about six at a time as reining-back can be a great strain on the horse.

BHS Elementary Test 23

A, Enter at working trot

I make sure that my horse is balanced and active before entering at A and that the contact with leg and hand are even.

X, Halt Salute, C, Track Left

I like a firm forward-going feel as I travel to X, but some way before X I will prepare for the halt by using two or three invisible steadying aids to reduce impulsion, using my legs to make sure that the hind legs stay under the horse as he comes to halt.

The aids increase for the halt until the horse is still, when I ease both leg and hand fractionally, but not too much as I have to move off again and must not lose the hindquarters or the head position. I do not allow the horse to look round at the halt and be inattentive.

I use my legs more for the move off and keep the reins even hoping my horse will go straight between them. Before G, I prepare for the turn by giving a minor half halt and positioning of the shoulders all at once, and at C I track left making sure that the stride is level.

E, Turn Left

I ride the first corner with correct flexion and rhythm, using my inside leg into my outside rein which is controlling the speed. Before E, I repeat my half halt and positioning aid and make the turn just before the marker so that I now face B. I go straight for a couple of strides and then prepare to turn.

B, Track Right

My horse should be in the correct position to go to the right, then straighten and go down the long side. I will have transferred my control now to my left hand, using the inside leg to keep up impulsion.

I make sure I ride the corner, go along the short end of the arena straight, and then ride the next corner. However, before the second corner, I am preparing for the circle, shortening the strides fractionally to make sure the balance will be right, and positioning the shoulders.

K, Circle Right 10 m Diameter

I arrive at K, and begin the circle looking to see how big it has to be. I must be 1 m from the track after A having first touched the centre line.

I must then straighten and ride to E. Before E, I position again for the half circle.

EX Half Circle Right 10 m Diameter
XB Half Circle Left 10 m Diameter

The first half circle must bring me onto the centre line, so that I can travel down it away from the judge for a few strides while I change position for the left half circle. Both must be in the same rhythm with equal curvature both ways. I must not let the horse anticipate and swing the hindquarters. He must maintain his carriage. I proceed to M, preparing for the circle.

M, Circle Left 10 m Diameter

I try to equal the amount of flexion in this circle as in my right circle, not allowing any drop in the impulsion. As I pass C, I increase my leg aids a little to activate the hind legs more in preparation for the medium trot. Having ridden the corner I arrive at H.

HEK Medium Trot

I must have the horse straight by H, to make sure that the length of the strides will be even and that the balance will be correct.

As I ask with my legs for more length, I expect to feel the horse 'ask' to go forward which I must allow with my hands so that he can stretch a little. I do not allow him to fall forwards or drop onto the forehand. He must lift his shoulders and stride out and remain steady until I give him the warning aid for the next requirement which will be before K. Then I give my final aid at K, when he should return to the working trot. In that transition I must use my legs to put the hind legs more under the body, and at the same time check the speed. The rhythm of the steps must not change although the strides become shorter. The outline must be steady and the horse straight.

KAF Working Trot

I must ride the corners correctly and keep my horse active using inside leg to outside rein. The flexion must be slight so not too much inside rein.

FXH Change Rein At Medium Trot

At F, I turn onto the diagonal paying attention to the balance and trying to make sure that my horse is straight and aim for the track just before H.

I return to working trot while still on the diagonal and then make the turn onto the track just before H.

I collect the stride a little to prepare for the halt, sit and close my legs to keep the hind legs under the horse and I give the halt aid so that I stop as my leg is beside C.

C, Halt Immobility Six Seconds

I freeze – trying to be relaxed yet ready to control anything which moves. My legs are resting against the horse's sides, and my contact does not exceed my leg pressure as this may make him step back. I have aimed at being straight and I have hoped that he has halted square. If I can feel anything wrong I will try to correct this before the immobility starts.

The six seconds over, I squeeze and ease and he should be attentive and go straight into walk. I allow the strides to go forward with as little interference as possible. I ride the corner.

MXK

At M, I turn onto the diagonal and let him take the rein forward. I keep contact but must not stop the stretching. I keep him straight and although I squeeze with my legs, I try not to hurry him and rush the stride which must feel long and purposeful. I take up the rein before K, slowly so as not to change the strides, and take a firmer contact.

90

K, Medium Walk

I turn onto the track and ride the corner using it to collect and position for canter.

Before A, Working Canter

I give the canter aid hoping I have enough impulsion to get me into canter without trot. I ride the corner.

FBM

Two loops, each loop to be 2 m diameter in from the track and touching at B.

At F, I ride off the track keeping my flexion to the leading leg and, half way between F and B, I turn back towards B, still keeping flexion left and sitting heavier to that side with my right leg well back. I try to control the balance.

At B, I repeat the exercise riding in again and, half way between B and M, returning to the track. I must make sure I do not lose balance and change leg, lose the bend to the leading leg, or get into a yield by mistake.

I ride the corner.

C, Circle Left 15 m Diameter

I go forward a little more and ease the impulsion which was necessarily very controlled for the loops. I must remember this is 15 m and therefore I must be 2½ m in from the track each side, and I do not go through X.

I ride the corner.

HXF Change The Rein With Change Of Leg
Through Trot At X

At H, I turn onto the diagonal keeping the horse positioned to the leading leg. Before X, I check the speed, if necessary a couple of times, to make sure that the hind legs will carry the horse in the transition, and that he will not fall heavily on the forehand. The transition must be straight and his head must be steady.

As soon as he is in trot I position for right canter and then ask for the strike off. I hope to have only trotted a few strides at X, and that the transitions from and to canter have occurred at equal distance either side of X.

I ride the corner.

A, Circle Right 15 m Diameter

I try to remember the correct size and keep the bend, but not overbending the neck.

The Corner
KEH

Two loops each 2 m in from track touching at E.

I try to do this in a similar manner to the other rein, keeping flexion, etc.

I ride the corners. I collect up ready to turn right at B.

B, Turn Right

I turn a little before B and aim for E, keeping straight and immediately give the aid for trot, and then again for walk so that by X, I am walking.

X, Simple Change Of Leg

I walk about four strides over X and then canter left, still facing E but preparing to turn.

E, Track Left

I turn before reaching E and begin to straighten so that I can go into working trot.

K, Working Trot

I try to make this transition straight and, if necessary, immediately balance the trot by using a couple of minor half halts before the corner. I use the arc on the corner for the turn up the centre.

A, Down Centre Line

As soon as I come onto the centre line I straighten and ride forward keeping reins and legs even. Before X, I check the speed.

X, *Medium Walk*

As I come into walk I try to relax and let the horse stride forward to keep him straight.

G, *Halt, Salute*

I ride into the halt as slowly as possible without very much impulsion keeping everything as steady as possible and letting him stand but keeping his head facing C, and I salute. I try to smile at the judge!

Then I ride forward to C, and turn right lengthening the reins but keeping contact.

I may pat him if all has gone well!

Part 4

Medium and Advanced Medium Standard

JUDGES' REQUIREMENTS
The horse should now show his ability to carry himself with controlled impulsion and activity. His outline should be round with a light and raised forehand, the lowered hindquarters taking the weight. He should be capable of extension and collection showing accurate transitions and greater suppleness. His balance should be steady from one movement to another. He should not be crooked and his acceptance of the bit should be such that the impulsion will travel through the horse and take him forward.

FAULTS WHICH LOSE THE MOST MARKS
Lack of collection and/or extension.
Hindquarters not sufficiently engaged.
Outline too low and horse not carrying himself.
Back not swinging, and lateral stiffness.
Insufficient spinal flexion in half passes and shoulder-in.
Crookedness in transitions.
False raising of the forehead.
Impulsion blocked by resistance in the mouth.
Wrong lateral flexion in counter canter.
Flying changes at canter late behind.
Dragging the feet in the rein back and wrong number of steps.
More spinal flexion on one rein than the other.

Collection – how to obtain the feel

To achieve collection ask the horse for shortened steps in good balance with the horse carrying himself and not using the rider's hands to lean on.

The steps need not, to begin with, be impulsive, in fact it is easier for the horse if they are not. They can be quite slow so long as the horse is not lazy. He must still desire to go forward and the step must spring not shuffle. When he has learned to shorten his stride and maintain the short steps without resistance and remaining straight, the rider can begin to ask for more activity of the hind legs. He should do this with the aid of the schooling whip, and not by grinding his seat into the saddle. The aim is to achieve lightness of the aids riding a horse with a round soft back. This can only be achieved by the rider's ability to sit with relaxed seat muscles.

As the impulsion begins to build up in the hindquarters, the rider can allow a little more forwardness but the horse must still hold the balance, the hind legs springing with more energy.

As the hind legs propel the horse forward with increased suspension between the diagonal pairs of legs, the weight in the hands may increase due to the impulsion. It must not be allowed to be heavy but corrected by the useof the half halts. As the forehand is restrained it will become higher, the neck arching and the head taking a more vertical position.

As a result of the horse yielding to the bit, the rein contact feels elastic and this feeling should be maintained by a feel and ease motion of the rider's hands.

Extension

When the horse is able to collect himself with the hind-quarters correctly engaged, he should be able to extend.

He needs the qualities that collection gives to be able to push forward and upward with the hind leg which will give him the lengthening and elevation of the stride necessary for extension. The picture of the horse when extended should be of lowered quarters and hocks under the body, not, as we sometimes see, the quarters high and the hocks out behind.

There should be sufficient impulsion from the collection to give the thrust with a slight extra squeeze of the rider's legs, evenly applied.

As the hands allow the strides to lengthen they will also allow a certain amount of stretching of the neck, though must not let the horse tip onto the forehand, nor permit any leaning on the hands. More weight in the hand may be acceptable so long as the mouth still feels pliable and not hard. The steps should feel powerful with much energy from behind the saddle. They should feel even. There must be no 'hopping' or unlevelness. The horse must be straight on the diagonal, or wherever it is required, before the extension is asked for.

The extension may come more readily if the rider goes with the horse remaining upright with the body. He must not mistake leaning back for 'drive'. Leaning back generally hinders the action of the horse's back, causing flattening which prevents the hindquarters from engaging.

If the rider wishes to extend on a diagonal, he must turn onto the diagonal, straighten the horse and then extend *maintaining* the same strides the whole way across. Many horses will fade after X, or shorten the strides before reaching the other side.

In training, the rider should practise maintaining the extension on the corner to prevent the horse getting too used to checking in the same place every time.

The extension at Medium level may be less than at Grand Prix level but the manner of the extension must show that the horse is progressing towards Grand Prix.

Making the canter straight

Difficulties in keeping the horse straight in canter occur frequently during training. The young horse, being naturally slightly one-sided will find one rein easier than the other and will, as a result, sometimes be difficult to keep straight on his bad side.

Teaching a new exercise may cause crookedness as the horse tries to evade his rider. Riders themselves are the greatest cause of crookedness because they may not sit straight, or they have may have made the horse's muscles develop unevenly by riding more on one rein than the other.

If diagonals are not changed frequently in trot, or if the horse is allowed to favour a particular leg in canter, then he may become crooked.

As the horse is a good deal wider behind the saddle than in front, when being ridden along the side of a school or a fence he will tend to put his hindquarters in.

Riders must not allow a horse to hug the side of the school with his outside shoulder. Room must be allowed for the hindquarters. If the rider can think of a very small shoulder-in position then the forehand will be controlled, and brought slightly away from the wall. The hindquarters will then be able to follow the forehand in the correct manner.

Whenever there is a correction required in the case of the horse being crooked on one rein, the rider must position the horse for shoulder-in until the hind legs are following the forelegs. Riders must take care not to overdo the positioning and must not push the hindquarters outward.

Flying changes

The flying change, to me, is one of the most exciting gymnastic exercises in the whole training, not only is it rather fun to be able to do, it also opens up a host of new exercises which hitherto the horse has been unable to do.

Some horses react very quickly to the build-up to flying

changes and will offer the changes with no difficulty what-soever. Others will find the whole thing rather puzzling and make a great fuss.

However easy or difficult they find the changes, almost every horse will find the change to the right or left more difficult to start with. It is surprising that usually it is to the right that most horses will labour.

Before the change can be effected, the rider must have made sure that he has taught two things clearly.

Firstly, the canter itself must be correct. The horse cannot change if he is unbalanced, crooked, hollow, or lacking in suspension between the strides.

Secondly, he must answer the aids easily without hesit-ation for the ordinary strike off to each leg.

The rider may decide to work up to the changes via the canter, walk, canter method, which means that the walk part between the canters is gradually reduced until there is only one stride, and then finally no strides, as the change is asked for.

If the canter is good and the rider experienced he may not do this, but will ask for a change when the canter feels right. That is to say, when the balance and suspension are correct. Quite often changes will occur quite satisfactorily this way, but it is perhaps not so easy for a more novice rider who may be trying for the first time as it does require quite a lot of feel for what is required.

Changes may often be late behind. This means that the hind leg has not come forward at the same moment as the foreleg on the same side, so the canter will be disunited. This is unsatisfactory but may not be completely disastrous when the horse is learning. If the rider keeps the canter, he may be able to make the horse bring the hind leg through to a true canter, by the use of the schooling whip.

Gradually, the horse will begin to understand these aids and will make a true change.

Sometimes, the horse will change late to the aid. This does not mean that there is anything wrong with the change itself, but merely that it took the horse a while to interpret the aids and answer them. This will not matter particularly, as the rider will gradually be able to insist on the answer more quickly.

More rarely, the horse changes late in front, but this is usually just a muddle over which leading foreleg he is supposed to be on, and he will normally correct himself quite quickly, but an urging aid from the rider's inside leg will encourage the horse to go forward and correct himself.

The rider should expect the length of stride of the flying change to be bigger at first than the normal canter because it is important that the horse goes well forward in order to obtain a good change. The ultimate aim is, however, for the flying change stride to be the same length as the normal stride, so that the picture is smooth and uninterrupted by jerks or swinging about, which often occurs if the horse is not happy with the changes.

Halt from canter

The rider must first aim to be able to collect the canter to a high degree. He must be able, by the use of half halts, to shorten the canter stride so that the horse is almost cantering on the spot. The suspension of the canter must be maintained.

If the horse will allow himself to be shortened to such an extent, with no crookedness or resistance, then the rider may ask for the halt. If the canter is correct and the aids given in the moment of suspension, the horse may put down his undercarriage, so to speak, and halt.

There will be many difficulties to overcome. The horse, feeling the aids increase, may resist in the mouth, swing the hindquarters or beat the rider to halt, by dropping into trot before the rider is ready.

To overcome these problems, the rider must try to keep the canter going until he is ready to halt. Do not be hasty with the aid but hold the horse into his bridle with firm legs until all the ingredients are present, and position the horse in a slight shoulder-in.

Having finally achieved a halt, the slight shoulder-in must be released, so that the horse is absolutely straight. He must remain on the aids, the rider's legs still in contact holding him lightly to the bit. The hands must maintain the straightness and stillness of the head and neck not allowing the horse to play in the mouth. He must be still.

The horse, hopefully, will have arrived square, having had the hindquarters very much engaged under the body, so the balance of the halt should be correct for the move off, or the next exercise.

Half pass in canter

The canter must be well controlled. The rider must be able to maintain a slow collected canter, with the horse straight, balanced and accepting a slight shoulder-in position.

If the rider feels he can do this he can try a canter half pass. To start with he may ride a 15 m half circle at one end of the school, and then try to take the horse sideways to the centre line. Only a short distance at first, with very little spinal flexion.

The horse may, feeling the outside leg come on to ask him to move over, confuse this with a forward aid and he may increase his speed. The rider's outside hand must have anticipated this and be ready to check the speed and keep it slow. The inside leg must maintain the canter and keep the spinal flexion. The inside hand will ask for a little lateral head flexion, which will increase as training progresses.

Eventually, the horse must learn to collect and flex himself to such a degree that he will be able to 'bounce' sideways on short steps with good suspension between the strides.

A canter which is flat, long or on the forehand will make this exercise an impossibility.

Pirouettes

Before the rider can teach himself or his horse to do a pirouette in walk, he must first be able to collect the walk. As with all training the rider must consider at what stage his horse is, and for what degree of collection he should ask. At Medium standard the degree should be well on the way to Advanced stage.

When asked, the horse should shorten and heighten the steps. The rider having achieved this by the use of several small half halts making the hindquarters come more under the horse, at the same time making him more active.

The rider must make sure that he uses his legs making the horse come forward into the bridle, then he should check the speed bringing the horse onto shorter steps. He must then maintain the short steps and at the designated marker the rider must bring the forehand round while keeping the hindquarters by the marker.

He does this by leading the forehand round with the inside hand, with the outside rein to the neck. The inside leg must maintain the lateral flexion to the direction in which the horse is moving and keep the horse forward to the bridle. The outside leg being behind the girth prevents the hindquarters swinging out and encourages the horse to step sideways and round.

The rider must beware of bending the neck too much which will prevent the turn being accomplished correctly. He must not allow the horse to step backwards. He must feel the outside foreleg stepping in front of the inside foreleg. He should try to feel whether the hind feet are static or whether the horse is picking up each hind foot as he turns, which he should do, to remain active.

Rider and horse may learn more readily by attempting a few steps only to begin with. They may try most easily by riding from, for example, K to X and X to F (see Fig. 14). In this way only a few steps are asked for at X, and the rider must gain a better degree of control by riding the horse straight to X, and then having to bring him onto a straight

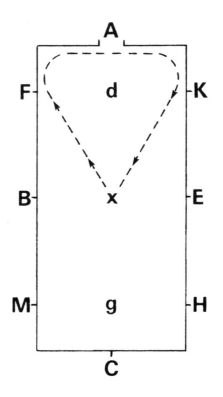

Fig. 14 Introducing horse to pirouettes

line again to F, after his turn. When the control over the hindquarters is satisfactory he may increase the number of steps so that he heads towards A, and finally completing the 180 degree turn to face K.

The rider may begin the canter pirouette in exactly the same way. As in walk, he must collect the canter to a high degree, really achieve some short steps almost on the spot, but never losing the canter three-time beat, nor the impulsion. He should try to attain this 'collection plus' on the straight at first, being quite sure that the horse remains straight. The hindquarters may swing, or the horse may put more weight on one shoulder than the other.

The rider should be able to keep a shoulder-in position in

canter. When the canter is short enough and controlled, the rider may attempt a few strides of canter from K to X and X to F (see Fig. 14). In this way he will only have to ask for about three strides of pirouette at X. He may then increase the distance of the turn gradually in a similar way to the walk.

Direct transitions (simple change)

Transitions from walk to canter or vice versa are required from Elementary upwards, and where these are asked for, the horse must respond without intermediary steps of trot.

To start with, the horse will not have the balance to be able to make the transitions direct and the rider may allow a few steps of trot. He must endeavour to reduce the trot steps gradually, by means of the collecting aids of the half halt, until the horse's balance is such that he will be able to respond to the rider easily.

To achieve walk to canter the rider must first collect the walk. This means that the horse must have learned to shorten his stride in the walk and accept this without resistance. When he will do this the rider must then position him for the strike off by placing his legs in position and organising the correct lateral flexion. Then he will give the aid for the canter by using the inside leg firmly on the girth. The horse, being used to the inside leg being the forward driving leg should immediately strike off, the outside leg having told him which leg to strike off with. The hands must prevent the horse from rushing forward and must gently restrain him until the canter aid is answered. As soon as the strike off is made, the rider must ensure that the canter is forward. If there is any restriction, the horse will be unable to proceed.

The downward transition from the canter to walk will be more difficult and will take longer to achieve precisely. The canter must now be collected to quite a high degree, the horse able to 'sit' with his hind legs well under the body.

The rider must use a series of half halts to reduce the canter until the horse feels 'short' enough to be asked to walk. When the horse is learning this he should be asked to carry out this transition on very level ground, certainly not downhill which will tip him onto his forehand.

As soon as walk is achieved, the horse must be allowed to move forward onto a good stride. He must not be kept in short walk which will cause tension in the back and other difficulties.

Where there are direct transitions across a diagonal into walk before X, and strike off after X, the whole sequence must be straight, each transition being thought about separately and very carefully prepared by the rider so that the horse is in the correct position to respond.

Medium and extended gaits

In Medium standard dressage tests the medium and extended gaits must show a clear difference from the working gaits and also a clear difference from each other. In other words, the lengthening shown for medium gaits must be lengthening toward extension, but the rider must leave a little in hand for the extensions themselves.

At first the medium trot and canter will feel like extension and the rider may wonder how he can arrange to show any more. However if the collection in the various gaits can be relied on, in balance and steadiness, the horse will then be able to move forward more impulsively, onto a bigger stride, without losing his rhythm. The forehand will be able to lift and reach further forward, thus covering a greater distance at each stride.

In trot the rhythm, or lack of it, will be fairly obvious but is not always so clear in canter, unless the rider makes himself particularly aware of it.

The rider must be very conscious of the transitions at either end of the lengthening as loss of rhythm makes the movement ugly and stops the flow of the test.

It is not easy to make these transitions clear without being jerky or sudden, but if the horse will respond to half halts he will be able to make them more easily.

Riders must beware of bringing the horse from extension to a slower speed tempo by the rein alone as all impulsion will be lost and the horse can only fall on the forehand. In fact, instead of pulling the horse back to make a transition down, he should be *pushed forward* thus putting him into his bridle and bringing the hind legs under him in preparation for the next exercise.

Use of spurs and the double bridle

SPURS

Before the Medium standard is reached, the rider must have introduced the use of the spur to the horse, and the feel of two bits in his mouth.

Neither should be used to effect a result which may be difficult to obtain in the snaffle with no spurs. The horse should neither be driven by the spur nor should the head be drawn in by the use of the double bridle. However, when the horse will answer the leg aids lightly, he must be introduced to the spur as it is required in the advanced tests.

The rider must use his leg normally and in due course the horse will feel the spur, but will not resent it unless the rider continually digs him with it. If spurs are used by the rider to create more energy or to enable him to refine his leg aid, they must be used effectively. The horse must respond immediately; a rider jabbing his horse persistently with his spurs is a sad sight and eventually the horse will become immune to them.

Experienced riders may use spurs quite early on, but it is a mistake for the novice to do this as they will not have the seat and legs controlled sufficiently.

THE DOUBLE BRIDLE

Riders will choose the bits they want for themselves or with advice from their trainer, so I shall not dwell upon that. The fitting and action can be read about elsewhere.

The use of the double bridle is fairly common-sensical and, as with anything new, the horse should be allowed to learn the feel in a mild way, so it may be advisable for the rider to hack out in his double bridle the first time. The horse will be interested in the countryside and will not be wondering too much about the new things in his mouth.

As time progresses, the horse will be asked to work in his double with more pressure on the snaffle rein, to start with. Riders must be very careful not to catch the curb rein by mistake as the effect of this is quite sharp and may cause the horse discomfort which can cause resistance.

When the curb chain is fitted it must lie flat in the chin groove, and should not come into action until the angle of the curb bit is drawn back by the curb rein to approximately 45 degrees from the vertical.

Tact and care by the rider must be the keynote, as it should be with each new exercise.

Part 5

Advanced and Grand Prix Standard

JUDGES' REQUIREMENTS

The gaits and their variations must now show a great deal of contrast, true collection and extension, precise transitions and a high degree of accuracy and obedience. The method of training must not have spoilt the natural gaits which must still be true.

The horse's ability to perform the tests must come from complete submission to the hand and leg.

The forehand, which must be light and carried by the lowered hindquarters, must be followed by a soft back, the suppleness of which can show a high degree of lateral flexion.

The development and engagement of the hindquarters enables the horse to operate powerfully and project himself forward with tremendous control and energy.

The impression is one of muscular strength, agility and obedience, the horse and rider blending together as 'question and answer' are given almost imperceptibly. Only if the right relationship has been formed will horse and rider achieve this result.

The picture will be gymnastic but also artistic, the blending to perfection of horse and rider being the ultimate aim of all who aspire to ride top class dressage.

FAULTS WHICH LOSE THE MOST MARKS
Insufficient collection.
Balance lost.
Halts and transitions not direct from canter.
Canter changes late behind and/or late to the aid.
Mistakes in consecutive changes.
Unlevel passage.
Stepping back in piaffe.
Insufficient number of steps in rein back.
Insufficient number of steps in half pass zig zags.
Loss of rhythm/balance in canter pirouettes.
Rearing round and too large canter pirouettes.

Beginning piaffe

The ability of the horse to shorten his steps and lower his hindquarters is essential to the development of his training. By teaching piaffe the horse learns to transfer more weight onto the hindquarters, bring the hind legs actively under his body, and raise his forehand. Experienced trainers will know from the feel or will see how soon to start teaching the horse the piaffe to use it for this purpose.

The less experienced rider should begin by first shortening the walk steps, until the horse will feel as though he would like to trot, but instead of taking a stride forward he will bounce up and down almost on the spot with a little forward progression.

The rider must ensure that the horse is straight, does not become tense due to the increased aids of the rider, and remains in a fairly slow and regular rhythm. He must not come above or behind the bit. The rider should maintain an even contact, allowing the horse to proceed forward slowly using half halts to prevent him trying to dash forward. The legs should tap gently in the rhythm of a very slow trot, and if necessary the schooling whip applied in the same rhythm as the legs, to obtain greater reaction from the hind legs. The body must remain upright, the balance even on both seat bones, the seat muscles relaxed and the body absorbing the movement of the horse.

The horse must begin to change from the four-time walk into two-time, using his legs diagonally (as for trot) and spring from one diagonal to the other. He should flex his head more at the poll, arching his neck. His back must not flatten, but must lift under the rider. The hind legs must flex more and be very active without haste.

Beginning in walk, asking for a few steps of forward piaffe and then returning to walk will help to keep the horse calm and will also enable the rider to control the steps more easily.

When the horse will accept these preliminary aids, and can perform a few steps at a time, the rider will find that not only is the horse developing physically as a result, but he will also be able to move in to all upward transitions more easily, and later in the downward transitions as well.

Improving walk pirouettes

The method of teaching the horse pirouettes was discussed in Part 4. As the training progresses towards the Grand Prix, all exercises will need greater perfection and improvement. The spinal flexion must be increased. The ability of the horse to step on the spot with his hind legs must be achieved. The outline must be maintained.

The rider must try to improve the lateral flexion of the spine from the work on circles, and from the half pass and shoulder-in. The horse must accept greater flexion through his length, and accept the positioning. He must answer the outside leg without putting his hindquarters against it, and must step round from it with short active steps. The collected walk will have helped to improve the type of steps required to bring the pirouette onto the spot. Half halts will need to be employed during the turn to prevent the horse finishing in a different place.

The rider must keep a good position with no crookedness

of the seat. He must use the hands and legs in unison to bring about the pirouette, not forgetting that the inside leg must ask the horse to keep marking time as a very slight and gently forward-driving aid. If he does not do this the impulsion will be lost and the turn will become stuck behind, or the horse may even step back, away from the pivotting hind leg.

Travers and renvers

HALF PASS HEAD TO WALL AND HALF PASS TAIL TO WALL
Half pass and spinal flexion has already been discussed, and the manner of teaching the horse half pass head to wall and half pass tail to wall, is the same.

The reason for using these exercises is to increase the flexibility of the horse, to develop muscles and teach him greater obedience to the aids.

Travers (half pass head to wall) is easier for the horse to comprehend as the rider can ride through a corner of the school in the normal fashion but instead of straightening the horse, he will face the head up the track and ask the horse to bend round his inside leg (see Fig. 15).

Renvers (half pass tail to wall) is a little more difficult for the horse because the corner is ridden and the forehand led off the track, similar to shoulder-in. The curvature of the horse has to be altered after completing the corner, to a lateral spinal flexion round what was originally the rider's outside leg. That outside leg must now become the inside leg as the bend must be round it (see Fig. 16).

Riders may find this difficult to ride, but first they must ride the corner, then ride the front feet in from the track and simultaneously use the legs and hands to change the bend. At first the horse may be quite straight until he gets the idea, but as soon as he will answer the change of aids, he must then be asked for the correct spinal flexion.

110

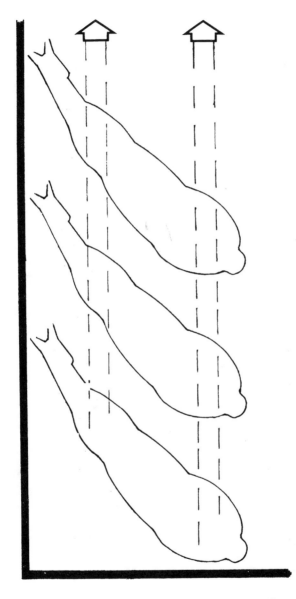

Fig. 15 Travers – half pass head to wall

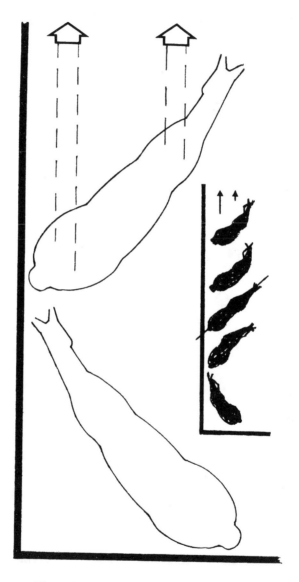

Fig. 16 Renvers – half pass tail to wall

Pirouettes in canter

The canter must first of all be brought to a high degree of collection. If the horse does not allow himself to be shortened to steps which are virtually on the spot he cannot perform the pirouette.

The aim of the rider is to collect by means of several half halts until the canter is very short but still moving forward. There must be no coming behind the bit as sometimes happens, nor resistance to the hand, which will result in stiffness and a lack of engagement of the hind legs, a situation which prevents the execution of this exercise.

If the horse has allowed himself to be collected to this high degree, the rider must also be able to position him round the inside leg, in other words, flex the horse in the direction he wants to go. He will adopt a shoulder-in position so that the shoulders are really under control and can be altered at the rider's will.

If the horse, feeling the aids and anticipating the turn, tries to fling himself round, the rider should be able to prevent this if he has the shoulders under control. Similarly, if the horse will not come round on the aids, the rider must gain better control of the shoulders so that he can make the horse comply.

To move the horse into a right half (180 degree) pirouette, the rider would collect the horse, take a slight right shoulder-in position and commence by indicating with the inside hand a little away from the neck, using the outside hand to the neck to effect the turn, also controlling the speed and maintaining collection. Use the inside leg to keep the flexion and the impulsion, and put the outside leg back behind the girth to prevent the hindquarters going out, and to assist the hands in bringing the forehand round.

The outside leg will need to be quite strong to ensure that the horse does not swing the hindquarters out as he feels himself being brought round by the reins. The inside leg must keep up the canter sequence (the rhythm of the canter). The horse must not be allowed to slow down the rhythm, nor must the front feet come higher from the ground than in the normal canter.

The hindquarters must lower with the hind legs coming well under the body and the size of the sideways steps should not be too big or this will cause difficulty for the horse. There should be approximately four to five steps in a half pirouette, and eight in a full pirouette.

A full pirouette must not be attempted until the balance and steadiness of the half pirouette is established. If novice riders are not certain how to begin, they may try giving themselves a vee shape to ride, e.g. K to X and X to F (see Fig. 17) so that the point at which they ask for a few pirouette steps would be at X. They must canter into X on a straight

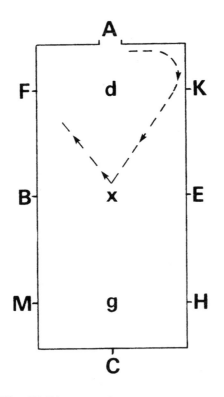

Fig. 17 Pirouettes in canter – vee shape

114

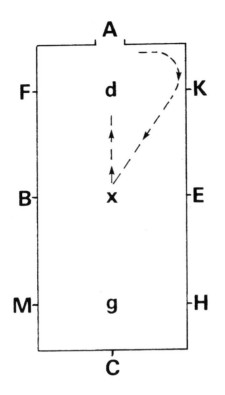

*Fig. 18 Pirouettes in canter – reducing the angle
leading to a 180 degree pirouette*

line in collection with the horse positioned. At X they will apply the aids to commence the pirouette until the horse is on a line facing F. Then the rider must go straight forward to F.

Later the rider may try reducing the angle, e.g. K to X, X to A (see Fig. 18).

Eventually the 180 degree pirouette will be accomplished, and finally the 360 degree pirouette.

The work on pirouettes must be carried out correctly on both reins.

Consecutive canter changes

The less experienced rider, training his first horse to Advanced standard, may be quite dismayed at the thought of making flying canter changes every four, three or two strides. Having just achieved the single change, that may seem enough. However, the challenge and excitement of trying something new will soon take over, and most riders discover that so long as their single change in the air is true, and on the aids, then sequence changes are really no great problem.

What will be a problem is to make these changes straight and calm as various difficulties can occur. One of the chief problems is that the horse may become too excited. If so he will become tense and worried and when this happens there is always resistance.

Lack of understanding is probably the chief cause as the horse cannot see why the rider is asking for one leading leg, and then the other. He will not react to the aids, so the rider will become impatient and the horse then ends up in a muddle.

To start with the rider should do his single (flying) change and not even think of sequence changes but canter off round the school and if the horse is calm ask for another change. Gradually build on this until the horse will reduce to changes every second stride. This should take several weeks as the horse must not be hurried. The rider must make absolutely sure that his horse is straight and balanced and will answer the aid at once. Most novice riders are too late in giving the change aid. They should count the sequence giving the change aid on the second stride before the change is needed.

The changes every stride are very difficult, and the average rider may need quite a lot of professional help to avoid too much confusion between himself and his horse. He should find that, if he can make a single change and as soon as he has given the aids quickly reverse them, the horse will almost certainly respond. To build this up to the number required in the Grand Prix will take time, but once the balance and rhythm of the changes and the speed of the aids can be felt by the rider, progress will be made.

There will be a tendency for the horse to either go forward too much, or to shorten his stride. The rider must try to keep the changes the same length of stride as his collected canter.

Counter change of hand

The counter change of hand, or change from one half pass to the other, is done in trot and in canter.

In trot, the rider should ride up the centre line and begin his half pass to whichever direction he chooses, after a few strides he should ride straight forward for a few steps, while reversing his aids and flexion, and then go into half pass in the other direction. Gradually the amount of straightening between each half pass is reduced until it is merely a change of bend and the change over.

Similarly, in canter he should ride straight forward after his first half pass, effect a straight change in the air, and then take the next half pass.

As the horse becomes more advanced the change will be only one stride forward and in the case of a specified number of half pass steps, i.e. 4, 8, 8, 4, the rider would ask for the last stride in each half pass direction, to be the straight stride for the change.

Difficulties can occur. The chief fault will probably be that the hindquarters will not come across correctly aligned with the forehand. They will lead or trail. If they lead, the bend will be very unnatural and the horse will have a lot of difficulty with his balance because the forehand is left behind. If they trail then there will be no real flexion and, as lack of impulsion is frequently the cause, other faults will also occur.

Riders must be conscious of true lateral flexion in either direction, and give the horse time to effect the change over when he is learning. Aids must be clear with good use of the inside leg to keep the lateral flexion and most important keep the horse forward to the bit.

Beginning passage

When the collected trot is thoroughly established, the rider may decide that he would like to ascend to the peak of the work in trot, and attempt to teach the horse the passage, a slow elevated trot with an extended period of suspension.

The horse must first show no resistance to the collection or the half halt. He must be able to maintain a respectable piaffe with lowered hindquarters, a light forehand and even steps.

There are different ways of beginning passage, some riders will develop it from piaffe, others will reach it from a super collected trot. If it is done this way, the trot has to be shortened, the rider making certain that the steps are the same length, even on both diagonals, and in a very exact rhythm.

When the steps can be held in balance without resistance, the rider may ask for increased impulsion and activity which he must achieve by a closing of both legs round the horse, and with the aid of the schooling whip if necessary.

As the impulsion takes the horse forward, the rider, then by the simultaneous use of seat, leg and hand will restrain the forward impulsion and, if all is well, the impulsion not being allowed forward will lift the horse and give him more suspension from the ground. The first step to passage.

The rider must realise that he may only achieve one step, literally, to start with and he must reward the horse. The passage must then be built up on this basis until the horse understands the aids and can hold the lift of the trot himself. He must be made to stay straight at all times, and the rider must constantly pay attention to the levelness of the steps.

Gadgets

Whoever said, 'there are no short cuts to success', was, I am sure, absolutely right.

Gadgets, and I do not include side reins used on the lunge in this category, are short cuts or, at any rate, many people tend to use them as such.

Some experienced riders may use a running rein, for example, for a short period of time or for some reason to achieve a result, but, although many people think that they use them for positioning the head, this is not always the case.

Any gadget which is supposed to help the rider to position the head carriage, and which can force the head towards the chest if taken in a firm grip, is entirely wrong because it is only the forehand which is under correction, not the back, nor the hindquarters.

When the gadget is removed which it must be for competition, the rider will have no more control of the forehand and the mouth than he had before and, in addition, he may have fooled himself that the horse has been working behind but, with the front forced in, this is unlikely in the majority of cases.

The secret of obtaining the correct engagement of the hindquarters, a supple back, and a correct mouth, is what we are seeking (or should be) as riders, and if artificial means are used, the rider himself is less than effective.

The two, rider and horse, must learn together to find the answer to true impulsion and lightness of the forehand and they will never do this with artifice.

Some experienced riders may use an artificial aid for a time to help them, when driving the hind legs further under the horse, to control the tremendous impulsion suddenly in their hand, but they will never rely on the artificial aid to merely bring the head in towards the chest which is too frequently seen in this country.

The pure artist will wish to achieve that obedience, lightness and harmony between himself and his horse by his own influence, feel, and dedication to detail at every stage of training, building a solid foundation upon which to progress.

Any rider feeling the need to resort to unnecessary artificial aids will be admitting defeat and falling short. It is up to every rider to decide whether he is half-, or wholehearted in his ambition to reach a very high goal.

Conclusion

To conclude, I have deliberately not taken the rider through a Medium or Advanced Test as I have for Novice and Elementary. If they reach this standard they will have understood the necessity of accurate riding of movements in the arena.

They will have learnt to position and prepare, and will know the importance of the correct speed and balance needed to achieve the requirements.

They will have discovered how to connect the hindquarters of the horse to the forehand and overcome resistances.

With this knowledge they will need the practice of test riding and then develop their own technique. Confidence will come from this practical experience.

May I wish all riders who desire to do dressage good luck. They will need this together with perseverance to overcome the usual frustrations when training.

Rewards are few, but riders will find that those they receive will give great satisfaction and will, I hope, spur them on to greater effort.

One final thought. Only the things which we learn from our own experience are those which we truly know.